HOW MUCH IS THE

Milk?

Uncovering Your **GREATEST COST SAVINGS** in Residential
Construction by **LISTENING** to Your Suppliers

KEN PINTO

How Much Is the Milk?
Uncovering Your Greatest Cost Savings by Listening to Your Suppliers

Cover and interior design/typesetting by Donna Cunningham of BeauxArts.Design
Cover design concept by Eric Waisanen
1. BUS070160   2. BUS116000   3. BUS076000
ISBN: 978-1-956761-00-9
Library of Congress Control Number: 2021919227

Pony Press, 13155 Noel Road, Suite 900, Dallas, Texas

ACKNOWLEDGEMENTS

Good mentors help your career advance. Great mentors help you excel in all your goals. The best mentors help you become a better human; they know that *everything* is personal. Everyone needs a mentor.

I am grateful to all the terrific people I've had the chance to work with in my career. They made me laugh, improved my skills, and shared with me in the unequivocal gratification that comes from building stuff.

A few of these good people were my mentors for a time and responsible for pushing me to be a better me, not just a better carpenter. Some of them steered me in the right direction when I was tempted to go the wrong way. Others just pushed me forward faster than I would have gone on my own. Thank you. Thank you. Thank you.

The following mentors were each inspirational to me:

Gary Hughes—my stepbrother who continuously watched out for me and demonstrated what it means to be a good human.

Al Price—A master carpenter. He was also my first boss, and as such, I worked on his construction crew from ages twelve to sixteen. I never stopped learning new things from him.

Mike Anderson—my high school wood shop and construction class teacher. I built three houses with him after school and on weekends.

Scott Dudero—my first boss in production home building. Scott really cares . . . about everyone.

Steve Seibert—A champion of construction operations. Steve was the production home building mentor that showed me how to manage eighteen job sites at a time.

Chris Kelly—the man who hired me at Pulte Homes and gave me the freedom to enact my unconventional supply chain ideas . . . that turned to gold.

Kelly Safis—my mentor who kept saying, "Write the book." "Write the book." "Write the book."

I am especially grateful to my wife, Akane, who was a book widow for much of the seventeen months it took to write this book. She is an amazing woman, and I am lucky to have her.

Every writer needs an editor. That's what I learned from the professional writers I know and respect. Whewww! I thought it was just me.

I am most grateful for my editors, who each contributed in different ways to bring order to the many thoughts, concepts, and stories that I wanted to get into this book. They did amazing work: Kirsten Pinto; Karen Steinmann; Edward Rubenstein.

Beta readers for *How Much Is the Milk?* were given short notice and only three weeks to read the manuscript and respond with suggestions for improvements. Their insights, inspiration, and candor contributed to the quality of the finished work. With sincere gratitude I commend them for their resolve to make a difference.

CONTENTS

ACKNOWLEDGEMENTS

INTRODUCTION

The New Guy 9

We Can Do Better 13

Ask the Right Question 15

Every Little Bit Counts... 17

Building Dreams for More People 18

PART I: THE FOUNDATION

CHAPTER 1   CONTROLLING CONSTRUCTION COSTS

The Current State of Cost Control in Homebuilding...................... 25

Searching for the Right Problem to Solve 27

Leveraging Supply Chain Management Strategies: Step 1 32

Measurable & Benchmark-Ready Costs 36

Don't Forget About Options & Change Orders........................... 41

Negotiated vs Open Bid.. 44

Final Thoughts: The Unexpected Happened, Again.................... 50

CHAPTER 2   THEIR COSTS ARE YOUR COSTS

Uncovering the Path to Cost Reduction 53

Let's Buy Some Drywall.. 56

Unit Pricing Transformation 59

Determining Quantities 63

Unit Pricing & Material Quantity Convergence....................... 68

How We Got Here—Explained 72

Final Thoughts: From Big Fish to Small Fish, All in One Meeting. 75

PART II: THE METHODOLOGY

CHAPTER 3 LAST MILE LOGISTICS

Looking in from the Outside 83

Less Tire Tracks 85

On the Back of the Truck 88

Scoop Them Back in the Box 91

What Else Can We Put Back There? 95

Final Thoughts: Pushing Tasks Up the Chain 98

CHAPTER 4 BUILDER-SUPPLIED MATERIALS

To Buy or Not to Buy? 104

Rebates or Real Money? 107

Appliances & Light Fixtures 111

Min/Max Paint 114

Private Labeling 118

Final Thoughts: Well Done 120

CHAPTER 5 JUST KITTING

It's Okay, We'll Finish It Tomorrow 125

The Multiplier of Kitting 128

Rough & Finish Electrical 131

HVAC 136

Plumbing 140

Final Thoughts: Just a Box of Locks? 143

CHAPTER 6 DEMAND SIGNALS

24 to 48 Hours Is Not Enough 148

Just-In-Case Inventory 150

Subcontractors 153

Distributor Signals 157

Manufacturer Signals 162

Final Thoughts: A New Team with the Same People 165

CHAPTER 7   Subcontractor Relations

No More Mr. Tough Guy 170

Listening Lowers Costs 172

Job Readiness 175

Podding Communities 179

From Plumber to Businessman 183

Final Thoughts: The Trade Council 185

Part III: Implementation

CHAPTER 8   Which Tools Are Right for You Right Now?

Assess Your Starting Point 190

Which Materials Should You Consolidate First? 192

When to Buy Direct and When Not To 194

Which Kits to Start With 196

How to Send the Right Demand Signals 197

Asking Subcontractors the Right Questions 199

Regional Differences 201

CHAPTER 9   For a Quick Win

Drywall Contracting Best Practices 205

Drywall Procurement – Quick Win 214

A Quick Win Through Consolidating Distribution 216

After the Honeymoon 216

CHAPTER 10   How to Make Cost Reductions Sustainable

A Culture to Support the New Supply Chain 220

It's Okay to Fail 222

A Common Language Will Bind You 222

Training: No More Winging It 223

Knock Down the Office Barriers 223

Get Them Out of the Office 225

All Ops On-Board 226

Culture = Character 226

Managing the Grief of Change.. 228

A New Definition of Team... 230

Right People on the Bus? 234

We Call It the Purchasing Department, but Is It? 234

Technology to Support Supply Chain Management.................. 235

Final Thoughts: Make Sure They Know Why 237

CHAPTER 11 CONCLUSION

From Cycle Time Reduction to Supply Chain Management....... 239

INTRODUCTION

The New Guy

J ust weeks into my new job as a superintendent[1] for a large
production homebuilder, I began to understand something
vitally important: Asking the right questions to ensure fair
pricing for all might hold the secret to excelling in this field.

Little did I know that asking a simple—yet vital—question
might be the key that would open some of the most exciting doors
for both me and my suppliers. But before I get too far ahead of
myself, let me explain.

Although I had nearly twenty years of experience in
construction, I was new to the amazing industry of building
people's dreams—their homes, their places of refuge and rest,

---

[1] A *superintendent* oversees, directs, and coordinates all aspects of a
construction project, ensuring adherence to proper procedures in building,
budgeting, and scheduling, following design and development specifications.

their abodes for making memories. And I was quite eager to make an impact.

Confident I could add value, even with no experience in high-volume production homebuilding, I launched into those first few days with passion. My new employer was a good company—touting high customer service scores and accolades from subcontractors. Now I needed to learn everything fast.

Regardless of my knowledge, skills, and experience, I was concerned that if I didn't learn the production homebuilding business fast enough, didn't meet expectations, spoken or unspoken, I might be out of a job. As a former construction superintendent in the military, my new job was to manage my community[2] well by keeping costs down and quality up, and adhering to tight construction schedules.

On time and under budget. That's what I was known for in my former position, and I didn't want to fail now in an industry that, for me, was to become the most rewarding of my lifetime.

I had seen great success while immersed in military construction, but it's hard to get fired from the military. Now in my first post-military job, I knew failure wasn't an option. I had a wife and five small children, and a determination to become the best in the industry. What hurdles would I face that, in the end, would catapult me to some incredible discoveries?

The first one came just weeks in as a superintendent with my first community that resulted in a paradigm shift for me and many others. Here's some details of what happened.

I was faced with writing a change order to one of my subcontractors and wanted to negotiate a fair cost for the change, just a routine step in the process, so I obtained a copy of the original contract and discovered it showed only a single lump-sum price. To determine the right amount for this change order, I wanted to compare it to the labor and material price negotiated

---

[2] A *community* describes the residential subdivisions or areas where the home-building company has contracted to build a series of homes based on selected styles and floorplans.

initially by the purchasing department, so I called them to find the missing pricing information.

They said they didn't have any detailed pricing. "Plan 1– $4,617" was the only pricing information available. I was confused.

The purchasing manager confided, "We only execute contracts with a single lump-sum price, and just do our best with it." I was stunned.

Later, I sat down with the purchasing manager and explained why I needed more detailed pricing information.

He went on to explain why unit pricing wasn't used. "It's easier," he quipped. "We use competitive bidding to ensure we get the best pricing, and we approve change orders as long as they look reasonable."

What does "reasonable" mean? I asked myself.

He said, "That's just the way we've always done it," as if that were adequate justification.

I had to assume they knew much more about this business than I did. After all, my employer was a well-established, successful homebuilder. Surely, they're the smart ones, and I just needed to learn their secret to success.

I was wrong.

Over time, I discovered that we were overpaying—by a lot, especially on change orders, and we didn't even know it.

I know how to do this, I thought. I know how to negotiate fair pricing and get these costs reduced so we're paying just what we should—a fair deal for everyone. I had just spent eighteen years negotiating labor and materials for every single project I had tackled, both in the military and prior, in the private sector. It's easy.

Still, this whole scenario proved frustrating for me, and I likened it to going into a grocery store that has no pricing on any of its products or shelves:

You fill up your basket with all the food you need for the week and proceed to the checkout stand. The cashier rings you up and gives you a total.

"Your total is $236.18, and you saved $11.44," she says.

Being curious, you ask, "How much is the milk?"

She gets offended and proclaims, "We don't use unit pricing." She adds that her company goes to great lengths to ensure you receive the best pricing and service, keeping you coming back every week.

Still curious, you ask, "Can you just tell me how much the milk is?"

She doesn't respond.

Is this story absurd? Well, this is similar to what we do every day in the production home-building business. Crazy, huh?

This experience changed everything for me. I went on to spend the next eleven years in supply chain management, determined to make changes that would ensure fair pricing for all. I'm pleased to say that each of the changes we made incrementally lowered our costs. In the drywall category alone, we reduced prices from $800 to $4,000 per house. In a later chapter, I'll tell you all about the division [3] where we saved $4,000—per house. Just on drywall!

The revolution in pricing begins with converting contracts from lump-sum pricing to unit pricing, but that's not where it ends. In the process of unbundling labor and material costs in each of our subcontract agreements, we uncovered cost savings ideas from subcontractors, material distributors, and manufacturers that led to more than 20 percent in cost reductions over the ensuing years. It's the rest of this story that provides the basis for this book.

---

[3] A *division* as used here refers to the local market operations of a larger national or regional home-building corporation.

WE CAN DO BETTER

It all started because I wanted to pay my subcontractor the right price for the additional labor and materials. Not too much—we needed to make money also. Not too little—I wanted him to be happy continuing to do our work.

Many of the most successful corporations in America attribute their success to the unique relationships with their suppliers—and we endeavor to be more like them. But if we're a company that doesn't know how much we're paying for the milk, we will never know if we're paying the right price. And if we don't know whether or not we are paying the right price, I would argue there is much room for improvement in our supplier relationships.

Where there is mystery, there is money—you're paying too much. But if you have the right associations, there will be no mystery. No money lost and potentially great amounts saved.

In an immensely fragmented industry, creating highly collaborative relationships with all the subcontractors, material distributors, and manufacturers in every location where you build may prove challenging. And unless a builder is devoted to making these soft skills a core competency, their best efforts at relationship-building may sit in danger of collapsing, and as commonly happens, they will often revert to their old ways of tough-guy negotiations and lump-sum contracts.

To those within our industry, the fact that we build houses with much the same processes we did seventy years ago may seem obvious. Materials arrive at the job site in the same manner, and laborers perform construction tasks using the same old tricks of the trade passed down from generation to generation.

Yet to others, looking from the outside in, it may seem like we are a well-oiled machine powered by the sophistication of modern technologies and systems. But many examples happening every day illustrate areas where innovation needs to take a center seat at the table.

In this age of a global economy and real-time news feeds, we witness companies all over the industrialized world reach remarkable achievements via continual improvement programs often enabled with technology. Our industry has not.

The Bureau of Labor Statistics reports that construction productivity lags way behind non-farm industries' year-over-year improvements. When you see a 1991 Oldsmobile Cutlass Supreme pull up to your job site and the driver unloads materials from the back seat and trunk, you don't wonder why. You see crazy modes of operation all the time.

The day I discovered that lump-sum pricing was chiefly used for paying labor and materials costs, I stopped assuming my company knew everything there was to know about production homebuilding. From that point on, I continually sought ways to use my expertise in cost control to make significant improvements to construction operations.

I confess to a prior tendency to give in to legacy systems. More than once they told me, "This is the way all the homebuilders do it," which was intimidating for a new guy like me. Never again would I assume that legacy processes were as good as they could be.

In the following years, I reduced costs in every single category of construction I encountered. My original promise to my boss to add a savings of *ten times my salary* to net profit each year became so vastly understated that we stopped using it as a goal. We made more money than ever projected, and we strengthened, not weakened, our relationships with subcontractors, material suppliers, and manufacturers—something I was told was impossible to accomplish.

This book will explain to you an alarmingly simple and often overlooked idea, one that promises to help you transform construction operations in a way that will motivate your suppliers to continually seek ways to lower your costs to build a house.

ASK THE RIGHT QUESTION

"Three bids and a prayer" is the phrase I attribute to the typical strategy of controlling costs of many homebuilders. They normally send bid packages out to three subcontractors, award the job to the lowest bidder, and hope for the best. Generally, no negotiations take place, other than hammering the guy with the low bid into an even lower one. He doesn't know he is the low bidder, so in his desperation to get the job, he will stretch his willingness to concede some of his profit margins and lower his pricing. It entails all the opposite dynamics of what negotiating with long-term suppliers should be.

I think it was the government that invented the three-bid process. I used to work for the government, so I have a pretty good idea why they do it that way.

The folks who work for the government are tasked with buying goods and services they generally don't know much about. They are required to procure millions of different products, ranging from lumber to parts for the NASA space program. It's not feasible they could be experts in everything, so the government developed a process to create a specific scope of work and/or specification for a product or service and then invite bids. In most cases, the government is obligated to award the contract to the lowest bidder. This method is not a bad system for folks who have no idea how much things should cost.

But in our industry, this three-bid process isn't necessary. If we have been building houses for twenty years, we should know how much a sheet of plywood costs by now. Three bids and a prayer may not prove as effective as some folks in our industry think it does. There's a better way.

Remember when I was determined to figure out the right price to put into that change order? I wanted to duplicate the contracted unit pricing for drywall labor and material to determine the fair value. I knew the subcontractor had calculated the unit pricing for labor and materials; that's what he used to put his bid together. When I asked the drywall subcontractor to break out his original bid so I could determine a fair price for the change order, he was shocked. He said that was one of the most intelligent things a homebuilder had ever asked him to do. He was happy to break out the pricing and help me find a fair price for the change order. In the process, we talked about all kinds of stuff. I learned a great deal about the drywall business from him.

I asked him, "Why do homebuilders use lump-sum pricing in their contracts?" He didn't know but said they all do it.

I asked him, "How does anyone know what a fair price is for any future changes to a contract?" He confessed this identified an area where he makes much higher profit margins because the builders don't know any better. He told me all kinds of things, and I was grateful for his candor.

Then I went a step further: I asked the drywall subcontractor if he would help me draft a new bid process that would separate out the pricing for materials and labor (unit pricing) for the drywall category. He replied he was happy to help. We worked together on the project for a couple of weeks, and during that time, he shared with me many surprising and helpful bits of knowledge that I could never have discovered doing business the way we had always done it before.

I spent the next several months sitting with each of our subcontractors in other construction categories writing new bidding documents. The result? Breaking out labor and materials had the magical effect of lowering our contract pricing. Additionally, the information I discovered during that process would later lead to even greater cost savings.

A false sense of security lies in the three-bid process that we, as an industry, have become dangerously comfortable with accepting. I have observed that three bids and a prayer rarely produces the best value in production homebuilding.

And even better, I discovered that *listening* lowers costs.

All I had to do was ask the right question. Once I figured out what the right question was, I used it with every subcontractor, material distributor, and manufacturer in my supply chain. I was amazed at how forthcoming they were.

EVERY LITTLE BIT COUNTS

One day, a worker on a job site noticed that door hardware and light fixtures get delivered to the same house on the same day by two different distributors. The question was asked, "Why don't we put door hardware and light fixtures on the same truck and drop our distribution cost by 50 percent?" I thought it was a great idea—a little crazy, but a good idea.

"That's absurd," I was told. Door hardware distributors have nothing to do with light fixture distributors. They are entirely separate supply chains with nothing in common.

Well, that's not exactly true. The end-user, a homebuilder, is the one thing they do have in common. In a typical construction schedule, both products are delivered to the same house on the same day.

Soon afterward, we had our electrical distributor bringing door hardware to the job site. Less tire tracks on our job site means less cost to our suppliers and lower prices for us. The details of this scenario are described in chapter 3, but I will tell you that between eliminating one link in the supply chain and combining these two products, we saved about $135 per house. That may not seem like much, but I was responsible for 4,000 homes per year at that time. That's over a half-million dollars per year added directly to net profit.

We have a tendency to hold our cards close to our chest, not letting anyone discover what's in our hand. It has worked for a long time, and some would say, "If it ain't broke, don't fix it."

I say, if you don't know the cost of the milk, you likely don't know what is broken and what isn't.

Some may not think that the cost savings potential is worth the effort it takes to make such a fundamental change to the way we do business. It takes about thirty-five subcontractors to build a house. Saving money on each one of those line items dramatically affects your construction budget. You just have to decide if lower construction costs are important.

From the time I worked with that drywall subcontractor to unbundle his lump-sum contract, I listened much more carefully to my suppliers. What they told me led to some industry-first strategies to attain sustainable lower costs—not just lowering costs for my company but reducing the operating costs for the suppliers and subcontractors that build our houses, too.

As we began transforming all of our supplier relationships, we set the grandiose goal of reducing costs by 10 percent overall. We soon realized that figure was way too low. While it may not be feasible to reduce the price of commodities by that much, few of our materials are indeed commodity items.

The production home-building industry bears a unique quality to all other forms of construction: repetition. And *predictable repetition* at that.

I believe that homebuilders have not yet begun to take advantage of the potential opportunities to leverage this area of our businesses. Some assume we have. Not even close.

BUILDING DREAMS FOR MORE PEOPLE

One day I was at lunch with one of the subcontractors who was utilizing my new door-hardware and light-fixture delivery process. Pridefully, in my own mind, I was patting myself on the back on what a great job I had done.

He said, gently, "You know, this is working much better than I ever would have thought. What took me sixteen years to figure out, you mastered in four months. However" (and this was the important part), "do you know all those costs we took out of my contract: purchasing, accounts payable, material receiving, material storage, Pick and Pack[4], and shrinkage? I still have all of those costs because all the other builders still do business the old way. All we did is lower my profit margins on *your* business."

This was a forehead-slapping moment for me. It was then I realized that unless the entire industry improved, a ceiling limit would exist on how efficient I could get. I needed to find a way to help the whole industry change.

Over the next eleven chapters, I will describe in detail the supply chain management strategies for reducing the cost to build a house. One of the things you will notice is how integral your suppliers are to this process. Your definition of "team" is about to change.

Figuring out how much the milk is should be first on your list, but it won't be the last. I started out thinking unit pricing was the end game, only to discover it was a gate that opened up a whole new world of collaborative work with suppliers—which all led to cost reduction beyond my wildest imagination.

In the first two chapters, we will explore the state of home-building operations *now* and compare it to a vision of *how it could be*—including why this distinction proves so critical to make. Once you have read the Introduction and Chapters 1 and 2, you can read the remaining chapters in any sequence you like. The stories from my experiences are not laid out in chronological order, but selected to enhance, teach, support, or illustrate a particular supply chain principle.

Chapters 3 through 7 are the methodology chapters. You can treat them as stand-alone chapters after you have read the Introduction and Chapters 1 and 2, but I recommend reading them in the order they are placed in this book. They describe strategies like consolidating distribution upstream, buying direct,

---

4 Pick and Pack, spelled in various ways (i.e., Pik 'n Pak, Pick & Pack), is the task of picking products from various pallets and assembling a pack of products to fulfill a customer order. All warehouses have a Pick 'n Pack operation to fill orders, a service provided so customers don't have to purchase products in bulk quantities.

and kitting,[5] all of which I think you will find logical and rational. What you once thought was too difficult, complicated, or risky is about to be debunked.

It is important to me that you have the information and tools you need to reduce construction costs immediately after finishing this book. Chapters 8 through 10 are designed to help you integrate the information you discovered in the preceding chapters.

One of the most common questions I am asked is what areas of construction costs to work on first. Chapter 8 helps you make that decision.

A methodical transformation of your construction operations may not be appealing to you and perhaps you just want a quick win, or you may want some quick wins while in the process of making changes. Either way, Chapter 9 includes a collection of quick wins, including a fully written process of how to contract drywall with fair pricing for all.

My supply chain management journey included the discovery of some methods or philosophies that didn't work. Chapter 10 is provided to help prevent you from making some of the same mistakes that I made early on. An entire book can be written on this topic, however, so I chose to include only the nuggets of wisdom that are vital to the success of a supply chain initiative yet are missing from many homebuilder company cultures.

Chapter 11 is the concluding story, rounding out the book's material that reveals my background, perspectives, and discoveries of how to build a house for less cost.

While the primary intended audience of this book is homebuilders and their subcontractors, material distributors, and manufacturers, I welcome all to enjoy the supply chain journey of a carpenter who only wanted to build houses faster. I

---

[5] *Kitting* refers to a distributor assembling various products on a pallet that a worker can quickly access and install. Compare this method to the worker breaking apart cases of products and loading what he needs in his truck, hoping he doesn't forget anything.

have included footnotes for terms that may not be familiar to those outside the home-building industry.

Each chapter includes actual stories from my experiences during my nineteen-year career in homebuilding. The pricing shown throughout is not intended to represent actual prices from any particular point in time but only to demonstrate the concepts. I have changed the names of companies and people to protect their privacy. The stories are followed by techniques and methods to help you improve upon everything I did. I'm providing you with all the secrets.

Keeping costs down is difficult. When times are good and home sales are soaring, material and labor prices tend to creep up. When sales are slumping, it's quite tricky to get our suppliers to back down on contract pricing as fast as our home prices are falling.

In 2002 and 2003, the company I worked for raised home prices by 32 percent in my region, and our net profit margins only increased by 4 percent. Where did all the money go?

Managing construction costs is a big job. Commodity pricing (for lumber, drywall, copper, steel, cement, etc.) changes daily; building codes keep changing, labor availability ebbs and flows, and weather can disrupt your whole operation. It's not easy to ensure you are always paying the right price.

Even though the tide of change will seem to push against your forward progress, I promise these strategies work. The cost-reducing methods laid out in this book are sustainable cost reductions—whereas tough-guy negotiations only last until the subcontractor can find a way to get you back (without you noticing).

Holding our cards close to our chest, combined with playing tug-of-war with subcontractors and suppliers in a futile contest, has gotten us to where we are today. This book will show homebuilders a different path to lower costs, enabling them to offer lower house prices and thus affording more people the chance to buy a home.

PART I

The Foundation

CHAPTER 1

Controlling Construction Costs:
The Current State of Cost Control
in Homebuilding

Aground-breaking discovery in cost reduction strategy. The biggest our company, our industry, had ever seen. Those phrases describe the innovative, new approach my team was expected to devise—a formidable challenge set before us.

Of the twelve process improvement teams (PIT) assigned in my second year of homebuilding, the one I oversaw was not only the company's largest, but it was expected to create the most significant impact on our profitability. The team involved fifty-two subcontractors, our top tier tradesmen, and a select group of our best construction managers—all collaborating together in an effort to cut costs by reducing the time it takes to build a house. As you might imagine, much was expected from this team.

As we were wrapping up the last brainstorming session—putting finishing touches on the final report, cleaning permanent marker from whiteboards—something was bugging me. Not just because our results failed to reveal the stellar, industry-changing revelation as anticipated. No, I anticipated that everyone would recognize the efforts behind this massive project, dismiss our team's mediocre conclusions, and assume our prior performances and processes already proved to be as good as possible. This project, if nothing else, validated the significant methods we already had in place. So that wasn't what was bothering me.

I was rifling through our notes from the sessions, searching for something that someone said during one of them. I couldn't remember exactly what it was, what exact point was made or what words were used, but I just couldn't let it go. I had to find that comment or remark that had left an imprint in the back of my mind.

I thought we might have missed something important. We were all in a hurry to wrap up and get back to our regular jobs. After three-and-a-half days spent in the training room, our team collaborating fourteen hours a day, while our email and voice mail overflowed, we were eager to get out of there. I had a feeling that if I didn't find the details of that specific comment now, I would never find it again. All these boxes were heading straight into storage, not likely ever to be seen again.

I found it. And then I remembered its context—who said it and why.

We had been discussing why sometimes our communities under construction have days at a time when no activity occurs for a particular house ... which led to a dialogue about scheduling and how sometimes subcontractors come to the job site that's not yet ready. Or, the preceding subcontractor's work is not complete enough to allow a steady workflow. After much deliberation, the group concluded that the root cause preventing cycle-time reduction lay in not having *the right person ... in the right place ... at the right time.* We concluded it was merely a scheduling issue.

Then Miguel, one of our subcontractors, said something that elicited a light chuckle, and we moved on. Yet, we shouldn't have moved on. The point the worker was making was actually right on the money, and it was important. Thankfully, someone captured it in the notes.

While everyone was cleaning up, I sat and stared at that note, wondering if it were nothing—or everything.

It wasn't nothing, I decided.

At that moment, I realized we were going to need to gather another PIT team and dive back deeper into some strategic brainstorming. Little did I know that this process improvement initiative would play out more significantly than any of us could have imagined at the time. The note on that nearly lost piece of paper forms the basis for this chapter. Looking back, it also marked a hinge point in my career and the threshold of a crucial change to our industry.

SEARCHING FOR THE RIGHT PROBLEM TO SOLVE

Before I reveal the exact words of that note, let me give you a hint: It had to do with finding the *right* problem to solve, the one that really swung the pendulum on a new and different trajectory and, subsequently, got us spinning toward some astounding solutions. Let me also give you some helpful background.

We had spent years diligently working on reducing construction costs. We employed every tactic we could conjure up and bring to life. Of all the ideas we brainstormed, however, the ability to reduce the *cycle time* of house construction always seemed to stand paramount in the goal of lowering costs. Then in one final push to lower costs, pressure mounted for us to devise an earth-shattering strategy that would blow the socks off the industry.

The result of this final initiative? "Just okay" is how I'd describe it. Sure, we shaved four days off our cycle time, but no one faulted us for the mediocre results. Still, I knew the senior managers had higher hopes.

This story probably seems familiar to many home-building companies. We all strive to keep costs down any way we can. Reducing construction costs allows us to lower house prices. Lower house prices enable more people to buy a new home. The more houses we sell, the longer we can keep our employees and subcontractors working. Bottom line? Reducing construction costs produces a domino effect that's worth the effort.

Yet building houses adds up to a massive endeavor of choreographed assignments—no small task. Unlike manufacturing, we have a product that stands still while the assembly line of construction workers moves around it. And we do it outdoors, subjecting ourselves to all sorts of weather extremes. So, *how do you make significant improvements to this industry* (which has been operating the same way for seventy years)?

This question emerges as particularly important, especially in an industry in which conventional wisdom primarily drives its processes. I've worked for four of the top twelve home-building companies over a nineteen-year career, and here's one takeaway I've noted: We all do things quite similarly. We have similar conversations, in similar conference rooms, with similar PIT teams, all engineered to pioneer a new way to outfox our competition. We all build homes relatively the same way, often with the same subcontractors and same building materials.

Typically, when a homebuilder starts up a new community, you'll see a mad rush to dispense bid packages so we can award construction subcontracts to the lowest bidders. Contracts are then written . . . signed . . . distributed. And then our talented superintendents are off and running, working with the selected subcontractors to complete construction on time and under budget.

Every subcontractor must do his part effectively, a worthy aim enabled by the on-time delivery of building materials. Yet ironically, home-building companies tasked with securing these materials have minimal contact with building material suppliers. We don't tell our suppliers about the products we have specified for our homes, the quantity we need of each item, or even when we will need them. But we often kick and yell and scream when delays are caused by materials not delivered on time. We repeat this process for every community, in every market, year after year. Wash, rinse, repeat.

They say you cannot manage what you cannot measure. When you award a contract to a drywall company for, say, "Plan 2– $6,216," how do you know if this price is better or worse than your last drywall contract? Plan 2 (or "Acadia" or whatever you name your floor plans) is going to be a different size and shape of home than Plan 1 "Magnolia" was. Managing contracts in lump-sum makes it impossible to know if you are paying the right price and whether it's better or worse than the last drywall subcontract you awarded.

In the graph below, Acadia is a single-story house, Magnolia is a two-story with volume ceilings and many arches throughout, and Kenton is a simple two-story. Yet there is no way to know whether you are paying the same price for drywall material in each of these floor plans.

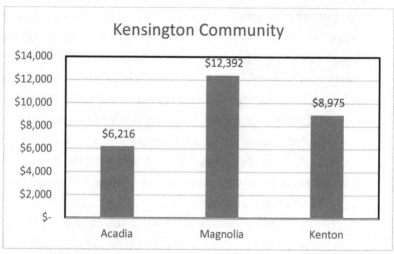

FIGURE 1. DRYWALL TOTALS

Home-building companies have grown content, resting on the familiarity of our traditional practices and knowing that our competitors are doing the same. Since the 1950s, not much has transformed in the way we build homes. Until now.

Japanese companies have recently moved into the US housing market, touting a very different idea of how homes should be built. I can assure you—they know how much the milk is. At the same time, other companies are improving the methodology to prefabricate intricate wall panels and bolt them together on site. Processes are starting to change, and homebuilders that still insist on creating houses "the way we've always done it" will see ever-increasing difficulties in doing so.

I think the days of three bids and a prayer are coming to a close. The risk of *not* changing is now looming higher than the risk of changing. And in these days, it becomes imperative to ask ourselves some probing questions: Would we continue the status quo way of doing business if we knew a better way, or do we know other builders who found a better way *and* sold houses at lower prices than we could? What would it take to inspire us to change?

Well, perhaps it was the message on that note—the one sentence that was nearly lost in the commotion of wrapping up three days of meetings in the biggest process improvement effort our division had undertaken. As I look back in amazement, I now see it gave me all the inspiration I needed to turn a corner into an unknown world.

Actually, the note refuted our conclusion that we simply did not have the right person, in the right place, at the right time—a scheduling issue. In a paradigm-shifting revelation, the note quoted a worker as saying, "If the materials aren't there, it doesn't really matter if I show up on time or not." The quickness of this response by one of the subcontractors at our PIT team meeting made me believe that he has shown up to the job ready to work but could not; the materials simply were not yet there. He was in the right place at the right time, but the materials were still somewhere else—the *wrong place*, in my book. Later, I discovered this to be more common than I thought.

During our high-spirited meetings, we had found it very easy to run right pass that comment. But I'm so glad someone caught it in the notes. My suspicions about that note were true: The key to making significant improvements to cycle time reduction lay in having the right *materials* in the right place, at the right time— *every time*. And, as you will see throughout this book, the efforts to make this happen lowered the cost of construction materials and labor, too. These changes come at an opportune time. Our industry needs these changes now more than ever.

Talent on our job sites keeps diminishing, and our ability to hang onto traditional ways of building homes is becoming more and more challenging to maintain. With costs steadily increasing and quality slowly decreasing, we no longer have the option to do nothing. The desire to sell more homes should be enough by itself to compel us to find better ways to build.

Thankfully, a solution is at hand. By emulating the supply chain management strategies developed by other industries, we can engage a more efficient and cost-effective way to build houses. In many cases, these methods prove more straight-forward than what we do today. Decades of continual improvement by other industries have revealed sophisticated techniques to control costs, and we need only apply these discovered efficiencies to the construction of a house.

Given that you already have the desire to lower construction costs and increase the production capacity of your subcontractors, you're already standing at the starting blocks—ready for the first step. This next section describes fundamental practices that will give you the ability to take advantage of supply chain management strategies that other industries enjoy. Some of the supply chain management strategies described in this book follow a specific sequential order of operations, and this next section lays out the first step for nearly all of them.

LEVERAGING SUPPLY CHAIN MANAGEMENT STRATEGIES: STEP 1

I want to introduce Step 1 by telling you a short story—and I'll try to make it brief. Several years ago, when I was a new regional VP of supply chain management at a renowned home-building firm, I went to one of our divisions to implement several supply chain solutions, ones we already had proved successful in other areas. In anticipation of my arrival, Sam was prepared with lots of spreadsheets; Sam was the division president and the former division controller.

"Cost control," he said, "is one of the things we're particularly good at here." He pointed to the low amount of variation in his lump-sum contracts and used the cost-per-square-foot of house living space to unitize his costs.

Sam's division was certainly high performing. Their customer service scores? Lofty.

Profitability? Higher than average.

And employee satisfaction? Couldn't be better.

This team was well-performing across the spectrum—Sam knew it and was proud of it. Thus, he was expecting me to respond in kind; he thought my esteem of their performance would mean I'd take my strategies to another division that wasn't performing as well.

And I *was* impressed. I acknowledged the great job they were doing and how much I enjoyed being around his staff. They were all terrific folks.

However, "We should try out one of the strategies," I asserted, "just in case it can help to further improve the already impressive metrics. It's better to try it out and discover its futility than to find out later that higher profitability was possible but we didn't make an attempt."

Sam appeased my request and called it a "pilot program." I didn't like the term. I felt I didn't need to *pilot* a method that I had used successfully for years; I was ready for full implementation. Yet, he presumed the great success shown in another division was because they were a lower performing team.

Biting my tongue, I agreed we would apply *one supply chain principle*, to *one construction category*, in *one community*, and see how it goes. I chose the drywall category. Drywall has few product SKUs[6] and a pretty simple supply chain. I also knew drywall would be simple and easy to execute, and would net some benefits. I wasn't sure how much benefit, but I was confident. Still, you never know in which category a particular builder in a specific city particularly excels. In this case, I was hoping it wasn't drywall. I had one chance to prove this concept to Sam.

Thankfully, it didn't take long. I knew the clock was ticking on Sam's tolerance of my meddling in his affairs, so I worked fast. Within five days, we reduced his drywall cost in that community by $1,200 per house. In the following week we applied the same principle to all his communities, with an average savings of *over* $1,200 per house. He was building about 600 homes annually, so

---

[6] SKU means *stock keeping unit*; think of it as any product that has a bar code.

his savings totaled more than $720,000 per year. Not bad for one category. And he had thirty-four more categories to go.

How was it possible that Sam, a division president so skilled at managing spreadsheets and analyzing variances, could have missed so much? How could both the construction department *and* the purchasing department have missed it? How come they didn't know?

Like other home-building companies, they relied on the competitive bid process to produce what they believed were the lowest prices. And since the pricing is typically in the form of a single lump-sum amount, they could not compare drywall prices for one community to those in another. Utilizing the cost-per-square-foot of living space, which some builders like to use, can be deceiving—as one volume ceiling in one floor plan and not another can throw it off. It's like saying a bathtub costs $0.11 per square foot (in a 2,800 SF house) instead of $320 each. Using the cost-per-square-foot of living space, that same bathtub in a larger house will appear to cost $0.08 per square foot (in a 4,000 SF house). Traditional home-building practices sometimes prevent us from seeing what we need to see. And while this may seem like the end of my story, it marked just the beginning for Sam and his division.

In another illustration, I once met with a subcontractor because I wanted to add him to our bid list. Surprisingly, he declined my invitation, so I asked why.

"Because," he said, "I know the subcontractor now doing most of your work. If I take one of his jobs, he'll retaliate by intentionally providing super low bids on my jobs with XYZ Homes" (the builder he primarily worked with). "We respectfully don't mess with each other's builder work." He told me that when another homebuilder pushes him to submit a bid, he intentionally bids high so he won't get the job and won't be asked to bid again. The builder, unaware of what has transpired, concludes that they already have the best pricing with no need to get more bids. The quick takeaway? Subcontractor interplay is an area of our

and thus increase your already tight overhead, just to manage this new way of contracting? I suppose all these concerns and more can trouble you.

Fortunately for you, someone has already blazed this trail. I had many of these concerns too, but few materialized. The beautiful aspect to this assessment process lies in how I've already eliminated the guesswork about what to do first, how to prepare, how to execute, and even how to structure your conversations with subcontractors and distributors.

If you've ever made a grocery list and shopped around for the best price, you know sometimes you will settle for a higher price if it means you don't have to drive to another store for just one item. On the other hand, if you just happen to drive by that store for some reason, you may pop in and get the better price. This process works much the same way—you shop around for the best deals and lock them in, but sometimes, on rare occasions, you must wave the white flag if the situation warrants.

So relax. I promise you, the decisions you will face in converting your subcontract agreements will be simple to make, and although not always easy to do, will be worth it. I'll show you how.

Now here's your first step in a nutshell: *Assess your ability to control costs at the SKU level.* Regardless of what I say, you have to be the one convinced that it's worth the effort to change. Or simply stated, if you just want to make more money, follow these steps.

Choose one construction category to begin with. Let's use the drywall category again.

1. On a spreadsheet, enter your drywall costs from each community for the past three years.
2. Then make a histogram chart showing a chronological representation of what you have been paying.
3. Now add the drywall pricing data from the same period from the Bureau of Labor Statistics (BLS), Producer Price

Index[9] (PPI) PPI #13 / #13710102. How does it compare? Are you consistently buying above or below the market, or does it vary?

	2017	2018	2019
Acadia	$ 6,216.00	$ 6,216.00	$ 6,450.00
Magnolia	$ 12,392.00	$ 12,530.00	$ 12,715.00
Kenton	$ 8,975.00	$ 9,300.00	$ 9,550.00
Ardoran	$ 8,915.00	$ 9,175.00	$ 9,450.00
Winterfell	$ 9,511.00	$ 9,511.00	$ 9,870.00
Greanleaf	$ 10,200.00	$ 10,315.00	$ 10,490.00
Willow	$ 11,740.00	$ 11,740.00	$ 12,080.00
Shanti	$ 12,360.00	$ 12,520.00	$ 12,710.00
PPI $/SF	$ 0.23445	$ 0.24660	$ 0.24840
ENR $/SF	$ 0.27480	$ 0.27549	$ 0.27554

FIGURE 2. DRYWALL PRICE COMPARISON

Now, if your drywall contracts are all lump-sum amounts (i.e., Acadia Plan–$6,450, Magnolia Plan–$12,715, Kenton Plan–$9,550), then you have no possibility of comparing drywall costs to the PPI, which at the time of this writing is $243/MSF[10] or $0.243 per square foot. The PPI provides drywall pricing for every month since 1994. I usually compare the PPI with anecdotal information from people I trust at certain drywall distributors to arrive at what I determine is a fair price for drywall. Looking at Figure 2 above, you may be able to determine if the percentage increase from one year to the next is aligned with PPI and ENR pricing, but there is no way to tell if you were paying the right price to begin with.

---

[9] The Producer Price Index measures the average change over time in wholesale prices of raw goods produced domestically, from multiple industries including construction.

[10] MSF = per thousand square feet.

If you can look at your drywall pricing and make a rational comparison to these resources, actual benchmark data, you probably don't have to change a thing. You're on your way to ensuring you are paying the right price for drywall, and you're eligible to employ supply chain solutions to increase your efficiency further.

If you cannot rationally compare your drywall pricing with the PPI data, it may be time to enhance your subcontract agreements to include the quantity and price for drywall material in your bid template.

I recommend starting with something simple and increasing in complexity as you get the hang of it. Drywall happens to be a simple category; you'll see I use it often for demonstration purposes. You don't have to itemize every single screw, nail, and tube of caulking, but as you become more experienced in unbundling labor and materials costs, you will certainly want to. For now, put the following items in your Unit Pricing page of the agreement, and apply this process to all your existing subcontract agreements, as well as to new contracts, too.

	Acadia		Magnolia		Kenton	
	Qty	Unit Price	Qty	Unit Price	Qty	Unit Price
1/2" Drywall						
5/8" Drywall						
Labor & Sundry Mat'ls						

FIGURE 3. UNITIZED BID SHEET FOR DRYWALL

Now, track your drywall pricing and use commodity pricing data to benchmark. Create another graph to track drywall labor pricing from one community to another. Even though the labor price will have some material costs included, as long as the line items are consistent from one community to the next, your comparison will be rational. Prices for labor and material vary by location, but once you have the benchmark data, your variance should prove minimal.

Three things affect the labor price of drywall: vaulted ceilings (requiring scaffolding), lots of arches throughout the house, and curved walls. If you compare the drywall labor price for a house with none of these factors to a house with lots of them, the pricing will naturally vary. If you keep these exceptions in mind, you can then rationalize variances in price from one floor plan to another. I like to group *like* houses with *like* houses to make my comparisons more sensible.

Converting your contracts to unit pricing will likely mean you'll lower your costs. I know that doesn't make sense at face value; it didn't to me either at first. If you're simply changing a lump-sum price to a unit price, why would that affect the total cost? You would think it's merely a mathematical conversion equaling the same total amount. Lower prices was an unexpected surprise.

And what's even better, the exercise of converting to unit-price contracts that likely will produce lower costs is just the beginning. The enabling effect of this process gives way to a broader set of methods to further control costs, making it even more worthwhile.

Now, sit down as a team and identify the construction categories that you think might be the simplest to tackle first. Just name a few at a time. In doing so, begin by exploring your team's expertise. If you have someone particularly knowledgeable in roofing, put roofing on the list. Generally, the starting categories I recommend include the following: drywall, light fixtures, appliances, flooring, and roofing. Then go after plumbing, electrical, HVAC, and framing after you get the hang of doing more straightforward categories.

Even before you exercise your new capabilities with advanced supply chain management solutions, you can do a few tricks in your day-to-day operations with your newly revealed unit-price data. In the next section, we will explore a few skills that will help your pricing and simplify the administrative burden of managing subcontract agreements.

Don't Forget About Options & Change Orders

While reviewing subcontract agreements in a division where I had already spent a great deal of time (converting most of their contracts to unit pricing), I noticed another improvement opportunity. Their pricing for standard options, late options, change orders, and extras were out of control compared to the base contract pricing they worked so hard to achieve.

Interestingly, they had done so much work over the past year to convert to unit pricing, seeing tremendous success there, that no one thought to apply the same principle to extra costs.

Homeowners enjoy customizing their new home with options the homebuilder makes available. Homeowners typically choose these options before construction begins, but if sales are slow, we often accommodate late-stage customization to prevent losing a sale. And subsequently, it's common for our costs on late options to come in high.

So I had this division ask themselves the same question as when they decided to convert to unit pricing. And I encourage you to ask it of yourself as well—in every aspect of your business that involves a desire to control costs: *Can I make a rational comparison of our pricing to benchmark data?* If the answer is no, you may have an opportunity to improve those costs. Remember, where there is mystery, there is money—you're paying too much. Solve the mystery and watch prices go down.

As we saw earlier in Sam's division, an opportunity to save $1,200 per house was easily missed by a high-performing purchasing team. Even after they grasped the process of learning how to utilize unit pricing, they still overlooked the open door to big savings. Since I don't want you to make the same mistake, we will now explore the next round of questions you should ask yourself regarding various additional costs outside your base contracts.

This summarizes your next step in assessing cost control measures: *Bring to the surface all the expenditures not typically included in base contracts.* This step often gives a high-profit margin opportunity to subcontractors because they know these costs don't receive the same scrutiny as seen in base contracts.

Usually, these costs arise at a critical time—while you are desperately trying to prevent delays in the construction schedule. More tasking added to a purchasing team already spread thin often doesn't get the attention it needs, and your subcontractors are well aware of that reality. I'll stand as the first to agree that additional work warrants a higher profit margin for your labor and materials, but keep it in check. I won't argue if you feel the subcontractor deserves more for an extra cost, just as long as you know how much more. No more mysteries.

Run a report from your accounting system to show all extra costs that occurred outside of base contracts. Pull all the contract folders for those costs, and one by one, analyze the additional cost against the base contract unit pricing. If out of alignment, it deserves an answer from the supplier or subcontractor. Sometimes, a legitimate reason exists for the higher costs.

Standard options built into the base contract deserve a slightly higher price due to their disrupting impact on labor and material management. The subcontractor has to order more or different materials, and his installers may spend extra time or need additional hands to complete the work. In the meantime, those crews could have been on another job, perhaps also featuring a screaming superintendent. They deserve a little bump in pricing, but not too big; having controls remains key.

Standard options selected less than thirty days before work commences signal a more significant disruption in labor and material flow, justifying a higher price. Late-stage customization agility can help a builder capture more sales. But while a great selling tool, it proves a big pain in the butt for the construction guys. Perhaps calling these late changes "non-standard options" may seem more accurate due to the timing of the notice to proceed. Late options may also deserve a higher price than early standard options, but as I mentioned, they need to be controlled.

In any event, watch this one—this scenario marks a point where the subcontractor will include a nuisance charge just due to the irritation factor.

Sometimes builders change the design after construction starts. Those of you not in the home-building industry may find that strange, but in the haste to get a community started, sometimes the design team has second thoughts and makes changes while the model home is under construction. Extra work incurred from these changes and anticipated on every house going forward should use the same unit pricing as the base contract. So watch out—this may illustrate where a subcontractor tries to interject higher-margin prices quietly. We can argue whether homebuilders should make design changes after construction begins, but the fact is, they do. Unit pricing aligns practices to ensure you always pay the right price.

Now identify the additional costs that are frequently negotiated in a hurry, and put a practice in place to prevent yourself from getting caught up in the moment and ignoring the cost control discipline you worked so hard to implement. Use your base contract unit pricing as a benchmark for these repetitive additional costs, and negotiate them upfront at a fair unit price. You may not have to use these items, but if you do and you're in a hurry, you can rest assured the pricing will be fair. It means a little extra work for you and the supplier, but it's worth it in the long run.

Cost control discipline proves difficult to do well and, therefore, entails another way to give your company a competitive advantage over others. By converting everything to unit pricing—all your base contracts and now your standard options, late options, change orders, and other extra work—you're on your way to gaining a competitive edge.

Copy and paste the same unit pricing format as needed from your base contract into the options and extra work items on the pricing page. Format consistency makes working with costs easy for your suppliers, subcontractors, and internal staff members. It won't take long for unit pricing to become your new normal—and lump-sum contracting a thing of the past.

	Acadia		Magnolia		Kenton	
	Qty	Unit Price	Qty	Unit Price	Qty	Unit Price
1/2" Drywall						
5/8" Drywall						
Labor & Sundry Mat'ls						

FIGURE 4. DRYWALL UNIT PRICE TEMPLATE

Now that you have unit pricing for all your construction work, you are ready for the next step. Your team will likely put a fair amount of labor hours into converting your contracts into unit-price agreements. So in this next section, I'm going to show you how to save some hours that will more than compensate for your purchasing department's extra time in putting this together.

NEGOTIATED VS OPEN BID

You deserve a break after changing all those contracts from lump-sum to unit price, coordinating with each of your subcontractors, explaining your intentions to each of them, creating new bi-lateral agreements, and doing all in a format different than ever before. Enabled only by unit pricing, you can now implement a time-saving process, reducing the amount of effort your staff puts into contracting, and start construction on a new community sooner. Unit-price agreements enable a comfortable shift from open-bid contracts to negotiated contracts.

Negotiating contracts can be scary. You've got the fear of not knowing if you're getting the right deal, potential ridicule from your colleagues should someone find the deal was bad, and the potential for someone to suspect unethical activity in your department. How could you defend yourself and your staff if your contracts were lump-sum? You can't. That's why unit-price agreements prove a necessary step before you start negotiating. Unit pricing can always be compared to other communities and established benchmark resources, taking fear and suspicion out of the equation.

I want you to ask yourself another question about your contracting process: After the architect finishes construction drawings and specifications—all necessary for subcontractors to bid effectively—how long does it take to complete all your contracts? A standard duration of time for bidding is thirty days. However, having all contracts going out to bid on the same day and then signed and returned thirty days later is uncommon. Usually, groups of contracts that allow the initial phase of construction to begin are done first. Then, while other groups go out to bid and final documents are signed, the duration extends to about three months.

Subcontractors taking longer to submit bids is also becoming more the norm than the exception. Most subcontractors are operating at maximum capacity and continually hunting for qualified new hires, giving them no time for training. And all the while, builders are demanding action. Many have admitted to me that they had enough field staff to do more work but not enough office staff to submit a proper bid on time. Due to a shortage of office staff, they sometimes pass on bidding new jobs.

What options do you currently have to increase the production capacity of your subcontractor's office staff? This key question stresses the value of considering your subcontractor's overhead costs as part of your own. If you could reduce his burden to bid jobs, you would not only reduce his costs but also increase his ability to do more of your work, presuming you are happy with his pricing and quality.

Each time you send out your drawings and specifications for bids, each bidder estimates the quantity of each material needed to complete the work. The required estimating labor is also part of their overhead costs and, as I hinted earlier, ends up being part of the builder's costs, too.

For example, you send bid packages out to three drywall subcontractors and give them thirty days to submit a bid, each for the same work or task. They each have an estimator who creates a bill of materials and finds the best pricing, extends the total cost, adds overhead and profit, and submits a bid. With three bidders, you are paying for the bill of materials to be done three times.

You may argue that you pay only for the estimating by the one to whom you award the contract. But they bid jobs all the time—sometimes getting the job and sometimes not. Bidding and estimating, all part of their overhead costs, is applied to all jobs, so builders are paying for all their estimates. If estimating were performed only one time, imagine the number of staff hours and expenses it would save our industry. This illustrates one of the reasons the whole industry has to change. A few innovative builders alone cannot eliminate the cost of estimating the same task multiple times.

Consider a scenario where you are starting a new community, and let's use drywall again as an example of how to reduce bidding, estimating, and contracting costs—using negotiated, unit-price contracts. On your last three jobs with "Donny Drywallers," you paid the market price for drywall, which was mutually agreed upon at $0.24 per square foot. Plus, he charged you $0.40 per square foot for labor, sundry materials, overhead, and profit.

On the next community, you call him up and tell him you have a new job, and you ask if Donny agrees drywall material is still at $0.24 per square foot. He either agrees or suggests a change. Either way, you agree on a drywall material price. Next, you say, "Donny, you did the last three jobs for $0.40/SF for labor and sundries. If you do this next job for $0.39/SF, I'll give it to you right now; I won't even go out to bid." He will then agree or justify a higher price. If his price is higher than your tolerance for the new community, you tell him you will offer the opportunity to some other subcontractors before you will concede the higher rate is warranted. In the end, he may decide to do it for $0.39/SF after all.

Drywall quantity is typically 4.2 x house-area square feet. For a 3,200 square foot house, there is approximately 13,440 (4.2 x 3,200) square feet of drywall. You may issue a contract for drywall for $3,226 (13,440 x $0.24) and labor/sundry materials for $5,242 (13,440 x $0.39) for a total of $8,468.

	House Size	Estimating Factor	Drywall Qty
Plan 1	3200 SF	x 4.2	13440 SF

FIGURE 5. DRYWALL QUANTITY QUICK ESTIMATE

	Drywall Mat'l	Labor/Sundry
Unit Price	$ 0.24	$ 0.39
Qty	13440	13440
Sub Total	$ 3,226	$ 5,242
Contract Total	$8,468	

FIGURE 6. APPLY DRYWALL ESTIMATE TO KNOWN UNIT PRICES

When drywall installation is complete, take a tape measure and clipboard and measure every wall and ceiling, which takes about forty-five minutes, and enter all your measurements, by room, in a spreadsheet. I prefer to measure everything in inches, converting to square feet at the end of the exercise. Now, total the actual amount of drywall installed, add 9 percent for waste, and you have the exact amount of drywall for your contract. True up the quantity in your contract to the newly discovered quantities, and you're done. With this method, you will pay for exactly the right amount of drywall, not an estimate that may or may not be correct. When your subcontractor knows you are going to be fair with him, he is more likely to be fair with you.

Community: **Pinto Estates**		Lot **72**		Drywall Field Measurement			
Floor Plan: **Kenton**		2,623 SF					
Date: **5/18/2019**				All measurements are in "inches"			
Room		Length	Height	X	1/2"	5/8"	Water bd
Entry		76	108	2	X	x	
Entry		52	108	2	X		
Entry	window	12	4	2	X		
Entry	window	60	4	2	X		
Entry	window	12	4	2	X		
Entry	window	60	4	2	X		
Entry	ceiling	76	52			X	
Entry	door	-36	96		X		
Entry	window	-12	60	2	X		
Entry	opening	-65	96		X		
Bed 3 Hallway		172	108		X		
Bed 3 Hallway		72	108		X		

FIGURE 7. DRYWALL FIELD MEASUREMENT TEMPLATE

I know some purchasing managers will hope for the subcontractor to make a mistake in his bid, forgetting to add some amount of square footage, and a lower price will be submitted. I believe that what goes around comes around, and if you plan on making margin improvements with this method, it will likely hurt you more times than it helps.

The subcontractor needs to order the right materials to do the work, so he will create his own estimate. But at least you aren't paying for it to be done three times. During construction, take note of the amount of drywall delivered to the house. Count all the sheets of differing types of drywall. After the drywall is installed and you have measured all the walls and ceilings, you can subtract that from the amount of drywall delivered to see the exact amount of waste. After years of collecting delivery and installation quantity data, I provided reports to the subcontractor showing him his actual waste factor and which of his crews were more wasteful than others.

Kenton	Delivered	Field Measured	Waste
1/2" Drywall	7000 SF	6017 SF	14.0%
5/8" Drywall	4400 SF	3959 SF	10.0%
Water Board	192 SF	169 SF	12%

FIGURE 8. ACTUAL DRYWALL WASTE

48

He was amazed. It was information about his company that he didn't even know, enabling essential training to take place with his installers.

So what have you accomplished so far? You just changed your thirty-day bidding process into a five-minute phone call and reduced the administrative burden of both your company and the subcontractor who bids your work. So you now have confidence you paid the right price. All made possible by your conversion to unit pricing.

Now that you've gone through the process with the drywall category, can you imagine doing it any other way? It's faster, requires less administrative burden, and nets a bottom-line price that you can compare to benchmark data and your other communities. In how many of your construction categories would you like to apply a similar process? I hope you just said, "All of them."

By applying negotiated, unit-price contracts, you have a chance to make a significant impact on your construction costs. Now, with these processes in place, you can analyze costs in a way that produces actionable intelligence. Over time, you will discover new information that you can act on—an immensely valuable endeavor.

Everything we have laid out here gives a pretty good summary of the activities required to achieve a higher level of cost control. Some categories are easier to manage than others, but they all can be converted to unit-price, negotiated contracts, contributing to higher profit margins and more consistent construction costs.

"If economists understood collaboration, they wouldn't teach competition."

—*W. Edwards Deming*

FINAL THOUGHTS: THE UNEXPECTED HAPPENED, AGAIN

One particular Friday evening, I think I was the last one still in the building. My purchasing agents had stayed later than usual that night, and we lost track of time discussing what had just occurred, stunned by what we held in our hands: the contract files containing new pricing sheets from our subcontractors. And they were not what we expected.

We had been working on our initiative to convert contracts to unit pricing, and each of us chose a few categories to work on first. The first round of new pricing sheets, formatted with the new unit prices and material quantities, were all due back from our subcontractors on the same day. We had invested a great deal of trailblazing work to get to this point, and now we would see the fruits of our labor—all anticlimactic as far as we were concerned. To us, this phase was purely administrative. As part of our supply chain management improvement process, we had asked our contractors to just convert their lump-sum price into our new unit-price format.

It's certainly not logical that converting lump-sum contracts to unit-price contracts would result in lower prices. My sole intention was to gain visibility into our actual costs. We knew we had to unbundle labor from material, first in a unit-pricing format, before we would even attempt cost reduction. I think I assumed that some of our pricing would be aligned with what it should be, and some, after benchmark comparisons, would present an opportunity to ask a new question. That's all I wanted to do. We were eager to get started answering the burning question: Are we paying the right price?

Without unit pricing, I never could have asked myself (or my staff) if we were paying the right price or not. It would have remained a mystery. As I told my team, we were going to do what it takes to convert to unit pricing . . . and when complete, if we felt that opportunities existed to reduce costs in a couple of categories, we would prioritize and tackle them one by one.

Yet that plan quickly changed as we started discussing the results memorialized in the contract folders we now held in our hands. Without any prompting from my staff or me, our subcontractors lowered their prices. It turns out they assumed we had caught them at their game, and they were conceding to a fairer semblance of the pricing they should have been charging us.

So there we stood in my office, all in shock that all our subcontractors sent in new unit-price proposals with lower prices. We had no expectation this would happen. And the shock? It lasted a good long while.

I think we reduced our construction costs by about four million dollars that year, and none of it intentional.

Soon afterward, I was promoted to regional VP of supply chain management and applied these same strategies to the rest of our region. Time and time again, every pilot we completed resulted in lower costs.

Assessing your company's ability to control costs makes all the difference in how you view relationships with subcontractors and suppliers. The most effective cost management strategies stem from an initial desire to see these relationships at root level. Realizing you cannot do so on your own just sitting at your desk, you then begin collaborating with your subcontractors and suppliers in a whole new way, opening windows of opportunity you may not have thought possible. You will soon discover who wants to partner with you and who doesn't.

And that's really the heart of the matter. Learning to collaborate with subcontractors and building material distributors in a meaningful way—with the aim of lowering each other's costs—simply made our jobs more fulfilling than ever before.

Clearly, utilizing negotiated, unit-price contracts opens a gate to a myriad of supply chain strategies, but even if you only accomplished that one step, you would prosper. My staff was capable of much more than three bids and a prayer, and I couldn't wait to see what they could do with this limitation lifted.

As I finished locking up the building that night, keys still in my hand as I walked to my car, I felt a new wave of astonishment wash over me. Pleasantly surprised at what had transpired that afternoon, I said one word to myself as I swung open the car door and sat down inside: "Huh!"

Words were few. But the sense of fulfillment and satisfaction left me feeling eager for tomorrow to begin.

CHAPTER 2

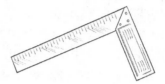

Their Costs Are Your Costs: Uncovering the Path to Cost Reduction

Minutes ticked by as we sat in the conference room waiting for one more supplier. For two days now we had been meeting with suppliers back-to-back. Yet what had we gained? We were in no better position than when we started and perhaps had even moved backward a bit. While we were nothing but cordial—never raising our voices, making demands, or even posturing—more than one supplier had left while making aggressive gestures and bellowing profanities.

We began this process thinking it was going to be easy. Instead, after two days, we were like two old party balloons: shiny luster gone, partially deflated, hoping someone would end our misery.

But then, just as we gathered the strength to endure one more session of abuse, a beautiful thing happened.

When the next supplier walked in—two gentlemen from GEX Drywall—we could see their emotions emblazoned on their faces. They were actually elated at the prospect of working with us and succinctly explained why: "Our goals and theirs were finally a match," they said. They had been searching for us, just as much as we had been searching for them. Who would have thought that possible?

Here's the skinny of what they said:

Several years ago, they discovered that homebuilders don't have a clear view into the drywall world, and thus, sub-contractors often take advantage of these unsuspecting builders.

Therefore, they created a business model designed to give homebuilders a competitive advantage by selling to them directly. Or at least, giving them transparency into real drywall pricing, including inside information on labor prices—for every major city in the US.

Do you think our elation now rivaled theirs? A goldmine of information had just opened as we sat there in awe. And then, as we candidly talked with these two gentlemen that day, we learned the back story to this answer to our prayers, now dropped in our lap.

GEX Drywall had spent a great deal of time presenting their proposition to a myriad of builders who, one after the other, politely rejected them. They were shocked and dismayed that builders did not jump at the chance to have drywall material and labor pricing unveiled. Our meeting today was their last attempt. They were about to give up and go back to doing business the traditional way. Then they walked into our office.

In the course of our meeting, we explained a little about our experience over the last two days, and they offered some insight into why we received the negative reactions from the other suppliers. It turns out that our drywall subcontractors had discovered what we were doing, that we were seeking someone to sell us material directly. These subcontractors then made threats to their distributors, saying that if they did so, then the subcontractors would never buy material from them again. Blackballed.

Fortunately for us, GEX didn't do much business in the residential sector, so these threats didn't pose a risk to them. We ended up talking for hours and learned so much about the drywall industry that day that we didn't want it to end. We were drinking through a firehose of information that excited our resolve to get control of our costs. And the abuse we endured the past two days? Suddenly forgotten.

Having spent decades working for drywall manufacturers, the two guys from GEX fulfilled our dreams for information. They told us about drywall manufacturing production capacity, self-inflicted shutdowns that result in price increases, and what manufacturers value—and what they don't. They told us all about the pros and cons of owning a distributorship and how we could work with them to create a more efficient business model, increasing profitability for both of our companies. We discovered the difficulties they face in collecting payments from their customers and got an earful on how poorly subcontractors communicate. We realized that on every major pain point they were experiencing, we could relieve nearly all of them—easily and instantly. I had to pinch myself.

When setting out on this journey, we were seeking to find a drywall distributor that would sell drywall to us directly rather than through a subcontractor. What we wanted was better control over the process and a money-saving solution that eliminated one of the middlemen, who weren't adding much value anyway. Our intentions that day were to meet with as many distributors as we could and then choose one or two that best fit our needs. As we assumed everyone would jump at the chance to work with us, we thought we would then face the difficult task of selecting the top two.

However, we were so wrong. We discovered that not just our ignorance was working against us, but that subcontractors were actively working to thwart our efforts to gain control of our costs.

That, by itself, was valuable information, further increasing our resolve to see this quest through.

In that moment with GEX that day, I came to understand something about our relationships with subcontractors and material suppliers. The standard by which we had measured the value of our subcontractors simply changed for me. Through this experience, we now viewed our relationships with our subcontractors through a new lens. What we had considered strong partnerships were now set with tight boundaries, and from this new vantage, we could see some were lined with cracks. We had simply been unaware of the limitations in these good relationships.

This experience with a drywall distributor—and, subsequently, with our drywall installers—gave us a new understanding of what it would take, internally and externally, to gain greater control of our costs. This new understanding forms the basis of this chapter.

LET'S BUY SOME DRYWALL

I'm glad those many drywall distributors affronted us. All we wanted was to buy some drywall. Without this experience, we would never have known the true nature of what we had previously considered as our very best business associations. *Trade Partners*, we called them.

Those we had relied on for decades had just given us an aggressively defensive demonstration, causing us to ask a far different question than our original one. Now, we wanted to know *why* . . . why were they so defensive? What were they guarding? We speculated about the answer: Perhaps they were overcharging us and didn't want us to find out. We were only partially right. The real answer was much more complicated than that.

Yes, this story is about drywall, but it speaks to a comprehensive, industry-wide issue affecting every homebuilder who is trying to keep costs down. Our reliance on three bids to attain the best pricing had failed us and created a culture of *Us vs. Them* relationships. The subcontractors and suppliers who were supposed to be our closest allies in the war against higher prices were actually our adversaries. And we didn't even know it.

Controlling costs in residential construction proves challenging. If we built houses on an assembly line with our own employees in an automobile-type factory, it would be a much simpler puzzle to solve. Yet in an industry with so much complexity, it's easy to rest on traditional ways to get the job done.

Whether efficient or not, the conventional methods of building houses remain comfortable for all of us. Builders are satisfied with the current process, as are subcontractors and suppliers. Yet at the same time, none of us are making the money we think we should, and homebuyers are having trouble affording a new home. Something has to change, *but where do we start?*

This turns out to be a particularly important question to ask, as I have personally observed multiple homebuilders trying to offer solutions the wrong way. The best starting point for cutting costs and offering homebuyers more affordable options has been terribly muddled.

When most builders want to reduce construction costs, they usually put pressure on their subcontractors to lower their prices, out of the goodness of their heart, and ask product manufacturers for rebates to reward their loyalty. Sound familiar?

I think most builders adopt this approach, not because of the significant results, but because they are not sure what else to do.

Playing the tough guy with your subcontractors may net you a lower price—for a while. Yet, as I have observed, they will get you back without you knowing it just as soon as they can.

I remember a large homebuilder who sent out a letter to all their subcontractors and suppliers saying they were reducing all contracts and current invoices by 10 percent. How do you think the subcontractors and suppliers reacted?

Well, many of them who worked for us, too, came to my office, showed me the letter, and told me what they were planning to do. They said, "Oh, yeah, two can play at this game."

They told me they would find any reason to charge for extras. Then when they charged the extra, they would pad the profit margins, making up for some of what they lost. They also said that when manufacturer prices increased, they would simply pad the increase to make up for more lost profits.

It became a game to the subcontractors, to reclaim what they lost without the builder knowing it.

Tough-guy negotiation strategies work better in the commercial construction arena. In the home-building industry—where you build the same house, in the same neighborhoods, with the same subcontractors, with the same materials, year after year after year—you will find that what goes around comes around.

The side with the most industry information usually wins. Subcontractors are streetwise and don't take too kindly to folks treating them condescendingly. When backed into a corner, they will bite.

Why do homebuilders risk so much on such a flimsy strategy? Don't they know that any cost savings achieved with such a method is merely temporary?

When a subcontractor gets pressured into lowering his price, he accomplishes it by reducing his profit margins. You might argue that when his profit margins get squeezed, he will become inventive and find ways to lower his operating costs, making the lower prices sustainable.

Yet, not so. When I've discussed this situation with many subcontractors, they say a different scenario plays out. In reality, they are already operating as efficiently as they know how. Now, however, you have just become their lower-margin business, and since they typically send their best crews to their higher-margin customers, you may lose in quality workmanship. Or time. Or both.

You might even justify your position for demanding lower prices by giving them more contracts. Unfortunately, their lower-margin business is still lower-margin business, no matter how many new contracts you give them. So in the long run, do you save money? I used to think so.

Here's what I've learned. Ultimately, by moving away from traditional methods of reducing construction costs—three-bids, frequent re-bidding, unilateral changes, and tough-guy negotiations—you can better realize significant sustainable cost reductions that will bring you closer to your subcontractors, not further apart. Some say that our relationships need to be kept at arm's length to uphold ethical standards. In the process, I think we may have distanced ourselves too far, much more than arm's length from those who hold the keys to the lower prices we seek.

UNIT PRICING TRANSFORMATION

Dave, one of my purchasing managers, came to me with some bad news that he knew I wasn't going to like—news that my strategy to lower costs wasn't applicable in his area. He indicated we would have to devise a whole new approach for his market and, potentially, other markets as well.

The two weeks preceding this revelation were spent in training, reviewing over and over the new process to convert our contracts to unit pricing, evaluating each of the programs and the lessons learned from each. The new method was complete and ready to deploy to other areas, like Dave's. All he had to do was follow the procedures, templates, and conversations that we role-played.

Yet when it was time for Dave to implement our new method, he was uneasy with the processes we set up and so resorted back to what he'd always done: send out new pricing sheets, demand the subcontractors fill them out as part of the changes to their contracts, give them a mandatory due date, and then sit and wait for that day to arrive. This comfortable scenario was opposite from the instructions he just spent two weeks absorbing. His due date came and went, without seeing any responses to his requests. When he followed up with each of the subcontractors, they declared they just didn't understand what they were being asked to do, and why.

So in my office that day, Dave emphatically stated the process did not work in his region with his particular subcontractors. And he seemingly held the expectation that I would agree and go back to the drawing board.

However, after asking Dave about the process he used, wanting him to describe how the meetings he was supposed to have with his subcontractors went, I discovered he did not use the new tools and training at all.

And because he seemed depressed about his inability to get it all done, I then felt compelled to help him be successful. Thus, I spent the next several days in his office with him, meeting with his subcontractors—one by one, all day long—and instead of feeling frustrated, as I anticipated, he was energized.

Once we started asking the right questions and sharing why we were changing to unit-price contracts, the subcontractors said it made sense to them, and sure enough, every single one agreed to submit pricing on the new templates. Some of them even gave us valuable advice on how to improve our process and templates. Some were flat-out excited about what we were doing, excited to be part of it.

In the following two weeks, Dave converted all his contracts to unit pricing and established a new task force made up of select subcontractors that wanted to be part of this new endeavor. And hallelujah—Dave's demeanor changed from depressed to triumphant.

It turns out that Dave never had any confidence that these new methods would work for him; he had just gone through the motions at our training sessions so he would appear to be onboard. His negative thoughts became a self-fulfilling prophecy.

Once the process was completed, Dave reported a sizeable savings. I think it was about $1,800 per house, an extra-cool result as it was not a goal of the exercise. This process was designed as an administrative task, simply converting lump-sum prices to unit prices that would ultimately add up to the same total amount. So when we asked the subcontractors *why* they provided lower prices, they indicated a feeling of comradery had resulted from the questions we asked and it make them feel like part of a team, instead of an accessory to one. They wanted to reward us for that. "Huh!"

Unless an organization is diligent in driving new methods and procedures, people often revert to traditional ways where comfort is king. Dave was doing what he was trained to do for the past fifteen years: send out bid documents to subcontractors with a due date, wait for the bids to arrive, award to the lowest bidder, and write contracts.

In my experience, *subcontractors don't care how much you know until they know how much you care.* (And, yes, now I can hear you groaning inside.) This observation may sound a bit trite, but if you treat them like the enemy, or like a necessary evil to get houses built, they will often reciprocate that sentiment.

The question that changed everything was not necessarily newsworthy. We sat down with the subcontractors in our office, one by one, and explained that our objective to lower *our* costs was first to help them reduce *their* operating costs. Presuming that builders do things in a way that costs the subcontractors money, we wanted to know what those things were so we could work on eliminating or mitigating them.

We asked them, "What is it we do that costs you money?" It took some time to get them to believe we were serious about the answer and that this initiative was genuine. Eventually, they opened up like dam bursting. Oh, boy, did we get an earful. That flood of information led to changes that ultimately achieved the very cost savings we were after from the beginning.

When Dave's subcontractors were convinced we were sincere about helping them lower their operating costs, which often took several iterations of implementing what they suggested, they became our most prominent cheerleaders for cost reduction. It became a game to them, with each of them a part of our new team, battling against high prices. Some were more contributory than others, but all added something, and the process never ended. The essence of continual improvement was now part of our new culture.

As I mentioned earlier, Dave reported an $1,800 cost reduction to his division president, and that came from a process not expected to change pricing. And while this happened for many reasons that we'll explore throughout this book, arguably the most critical facet lay in our ability and desire to begin asking the right questions. For us to have started this process with the assumption that we, the homebuilder, were the cause of our own high prices would have been an absurdity quickly discarded, likely with laughter. But it was the truth.

Collaborate with subcontractors and material suppliers by working together to lower each other's' costs, and you will transform adversarial reciprocity into mutual trust and respect, granting you valuable insight into actual labor and material costs. Then, and only then, can you begin to work on strategies to make significant long-term cost improvements.

In the next three sections, I'll show you different aspects of collaboration that build trust and respect, eventually leading to a sharing of cost reduction goals. Transforming an *Us vs. Them* culture proves to be a daunting objective, with tradition remaining your worst enemy, sucking people back in as soon as they try to get out. I will illustrate a few components that contribute to a successful implementation of a collaborative culture with your subcontractors and suppliers.

DETERMINING QUANTITIES

Turning your lump-sum contracts into unit-price contracts entails many different steps, one of which we have barely touched on. Along with those unit prices, you'll be needing the correct quantity of each material in your contracts. We call those *material take-offs,* or just *take-offs* for short, and they represent a quantitative interpretation of architectural drawings—which is then produced as a bill of materials[11] needed to complete the job.

Omitting materials or estimating the wrong quantity will often cause delays in construction and changes in cost. Change orders may have to be written and approved, likely interfering with the superintendent's goal of getting the job done on time and under budget. For this reason, creating accurate *take-offs* is viewed as scary by many folks as nobody wants to be the cause of delays and cost overruns.

You can arrive at the correct number of widgets for house construction in several ways. One way is to hire a full-time estimator to determine quantities for each of your floor plans. Or you can outsource the work to an estimating company. Some material distributors offer estimating services in some cities, too. All are acceptable practices and will deliver what you need for unit-price contracts, but I prefer a few different methods that do not add overhead costs to an already tight budget.

As a skilled estimator, I've determined quantities of all materials required for at least a hundred buildings, mostly all commercial. As few commercial buildings are similar to one another, estimating their materials proves far more complicated than for residential. I enjoy estimating; it's gratifying work. I would have enjoyed doing the estimating for my division's

---

[11] A *bill of materials* is an extensive list of materials, from flooring and drywall to caulk and nails, all used to construct a particular floorplan. It's similar to the grocery list you take with you when you go shopping. Similar to itemizing ingredients for baking a cake, the bill of materials lists the materials required to build a house.

communities, but there's not enough time in the day to do that as well as my regular job of running the purchasing department.

One day as I was experimenting with new estimating software, a program that promised to turn anyone into a skilled estimator quickly, I discovered something odd. I chose to test this software by quantifying the flooring materials for three floor plans in a community we currently had under construction. Flooring is one of the few subcontracts that traditionally includes unit pricing and material quantities, making this a good place to start.

The program was easy to use:

Simply click on a material icon, like carpet, wood, or ceramic tile, and click your mouse on each corner of a room. That's it. It leaves a color on the floor, coded to the material type, and tallies the quantity for each material, neatly lined up in a column on the right.

I then retrieved the contract folder for this community and compared the amounts shown in the subcontractor's flooring pricing sheet to the quantities my new software had determined. My only intention was to see if the software estimates were coming out correctly or not. Because, undoubtedly, the subcontractor's quantity estimates would be accurate, right? I mean, as the professionals in their field, surely their numbers were reliable.

But there it was in black and white. The quantities were way off.

At first, I thought the software was defective, so I did the take-offs by hand, using a pencil, a ruler, and some colored pencils. *Uh, oh!* The software was entirely accurate, not a flaw. Why then was the take-off so different from the subcontractor's?

All the subcontractor's estimates for needed materials were much higher than they should have been.

At that time, we were working for one of the largest home-building companies in the nation, who negotiated quite vigorously with flooring material manufacturers for aggressive pricing. These manufacturers guaranteed that our pricing would be passed down through distributors and subcontractors. The pricing, I must say, was outstanding; we got terrific deals.

But now, realizing the quantities were all too high made me think we were not properly taking advantage of the great pricing that our corporate office had so diligently negotiated.

I had a plan. I brought my purchasing agents into my office and showed them everything I had discovered. Then I asked Sophia, one of our purchasing agents, to call the subcontractor in for a one-on-one meeting. "Tell him you're learning how to do take-offs and that your quantities came out different than his, and would he please come into the office to show you how to do it right?" I said. Sophia is brilliant at her job, very intuitive and resourceful, but with an unpretentious, humble way of relating to others. She was the perfect person for this task.

When the subcontractor arrived, Sophia brought him into the conference room, where he began smiling giddily, so eager to help poor little Sophia with her first take-offs. I watched from a distance as Sophia opened a folder displaying all the color-coded digital take-offs with quantities in the right column, and one-by-one she compared them to the subcontractor's contract pricing sheet, which listed his quantities.

She asked, "Can you please tell me what I did wrong?"

His face turned bright red as he began stuttering, visibly nervous. Then he stood up, dismissed himself, said he didn't bring the right papers for this discussion, apologized, and promised to get back to her soon. Just like that, lickety-split, he was gone.

Later that afternoon, Sophia received new price sheets from him, not just for that community but for every single community—with lower quantities reflecting lower pricing. All this time we were patting ourselves on the back because of the fantastic pricing we had on flooring materials, only to discover that incorrect quantities were cheating us out of the pricing we deserved.

The subcontractor who had shown his hand so clearly with Sophia now explained his inaccuracies as an estimating error, which would never happen again. We did not assert any other reason for his mistakes. Well, not in front of him anyway.

This story demonstrates the need to *trust, but verify* any quantities that affect contract prices. Some construction categories, like flooring, are straightforward to estimate; yet some, like plumbing, are quite complicated. Accurate quantities prove essential to accurate pricing, but it doesn't mean you must do all the estimating yourself.

My favorite method of obtaining accurate quantities is to *measure the materials after the installation.* I like to use the subcontractor's estimated quantities to establish an initial contract price; you need something to create a contract, and then you can true it up with actual quantities later. Sometimes you true-up, sometimes you true-down. Accuracy is suitable for both the builder and the subcontractor.

Both of you have to feel like the process is fair, and if so—if the subcontractor feels he won't be taken advantage of through mistakenly low quantity estimates—he will be more compliant in helping you true-up precise quantities.

Part of the reason I like this method best is the relationship closeness it demands. It will change your typical conversations with subcontractors, allowing you to understand their pain in many areas: with material management, with suppliers that keep changing their prices, with backorders. It will ignite all kinds of great conversations.

If you manage this process right, it will become an opportunity for you to prove to the subcontractor you are concerned about his business, another way to grow trust. Mutual trust proves to be a requirement for most of the future steps outlined in this book.

Have your painter, for example, tell you how many gallons of exterior paint, flat interior paint, and interior gloss paint are required for a particular house. Then watch his crew paint the house, and count the number of pails he uses. Compare it to the amount he gave you. No matter how many times you build that floor plan, you only have to do this exercise once; that's the beauty of production homebuilding. Repetition.

Now go through your list of construction categories and choose those you think your team can most easily verify quantities for. Generally speaking, the most straightforward categories tend to be flooring, drywall, door hardware, light fixtures, appliances, masonry veneer, and to some extent, roofing. Once you do a few, they will all seem to become more effortless. It's not that hard at all, and it's kind of fun.

Quantity take-offs entail a major contributory element to all of the supply chain solutions offered in this book. They aren't as challenging to accomplish as you might think, especially when you consider using your subcontractors as your primary source for the estimate. They are already doing it. Then, trust, but verify.

I'd like you to write down which three categories you will start with. Those that seem the most straightforward might drive your selections, but my first categories were influenced by what I thought were the best relationships I had with certain subcontractors. I started where trust was already well established and where I was more confident that collaboration was possible.

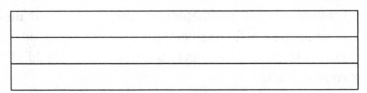

FIGURE 9. LIST YOUR BEST SUBCONTRACTORS

Now, we'll explore the next issue in creating unit-price contracts—the material pricing—and how you determine what is fair for the builder and the subcontractor.

Unit Pricing & Material Quantity Convergence

One of my purchasing agents left a contract folder on my desk for my signature. That evening as I was reviewing a stack of folders, I noticed this contract was a request for a price increase, a sizeable one. Recently new to this company, I had made a mental note earlier that month that the prices for masonry veneer[12] seemed unusually high. Juggling higher priorities, I hadn't looked into it yet, but now that I was faced with a price increase, it seemed like an excellent time to dig in. We were paying about $18 per square foot for labor and materials. Although a unit price, it was diluted with all materials, labor, overhead, and profit, so I didn't know how it would all break down. By now, you probably know how I feel about that picture.

Over the next few days, I studied the masonry veneer category fiercely. I met with manufacturer reps, toured manufacturing plants, explored distributor warehouses, and finally met with each of our masonry veneer subcontractors. These final meetings started with the subcontractors not actively doing work for us, but who wanted to, and finally with the two subcontractors who were already doing most of our work.

I felt I had enough information to have an intelligent conversation with our masons, and meeting first with the masons desiring to work for us sometime in the future proved strategic. I knew they had nothing to lose and would be more communicative.

Some of those I met with seemed more forthcoming than others. Some tried to provide me with as little information as possible, forcing me to continue with more detailed, probing questions. Eventually, I had everything I needed. I discovered that the stone materials were $2.50/SF (early 2000s pricing), the going rate for labor was $5/SF, and the rest fell into sundry materials, overhead, and profit. I surmised that 25 percent was a

---

[12] *Masonry veneer* is typically decorative stone applied to walls.

fair amount for sundries, overhead, and profit, making the total I should have been paying for masonry veneer $10/SF. So what was the additional $8.00/SF for, and why was there a request for a price increase on my desk? Did I miss something in my investigation?

Last of all, I met with the subcontractor requesting the price increase. At his office. His castle.

He was a large burly man, red hair, pink skin that quickly turned red when he was agitated, not one for small talk. When I arrived, he was waiting—with arms folded tightly across his chest, his face bright red, and steam coming out of both ears like in a Saturday morning cartoon. Holding my imagination in check, I made a quick mental note of all the exits, just in case.

In my calmest voice and demeanor, staying cool and collected, I laid out everything in the most nonconfrontational way I knew—everything I had discovered about the going rate for installing masonry veneer. I then opened his contract folder and showed his current pricing at $18/SF, along with his request for a price increase, and simply asked a question.

"Sir, can you please tell me where I went wrong in my investigation of how much we should be paying for this work, and please help me understand how to justify this price increase?"

He was FURIOUS. He started yelling, loud enough to rattle the flimsy windows of his office, banging on the table, and raising his arms like he was mad at the air in the room. I stayed calm and did my best to appear to listen, but my sole focus became the exits and which one was most accessible from my position.

After about twenty minutes of ranting, he stopped. I didn't say a word. A long uncomfortable pause ensued. I still didn't say anything. I waited. He went to the water cooler and poured two glasses of water, then came back to the table and handed me one. I was a bit nervous as he got close enough to hand it to me, but then he sat back down.

With his head bent over, hand firmly rubbing his head as though it hurt, he said, "You're right."

I kept quiet. *Best to let him do the talking*, I thought. He said that all my figures were correct. He brought invoices to the table to show me what he was paying. His voice was calm, almost defeated; he would concede to just about anything now.

He complimented me on my investigation and the accuracy and professionalism of my presentation. He said I was the first homebuilder to challenge his pricing. He agreed to change all his contracts to $10/SF . . . and then suddenly changed his mind. He said he would make them all $9.50/SF if I promised not to tell other builders. I agreed.

Those changes equated to $1.3 million per year in savings for my division. I later expanded that to my whole region and tripled that savings amount.

We need to know how much the milk is. No matter if you change your total contract amounts during your initial conversion to unit pricing or not, we cannot manage what we cannot measure. Visibility of both material pricing and accurate quantities proves vital to good purchasing practices as well as to other supply chain solutions covered in the rest of this book.

All I did was a little research and then ask my subcontractor to tell me where I went wrong; indeed, it was possible that I did do something wrong, and if so, I needed to know. How was it possible that costs could creep up that much without anyone being wise to what was happening? He said I was the first builder to catch him at this.

I want to add a word of caution. As you were reading this story, did your thoughts jump to a place where you were metaphorically beating the subcontractor over the head with this new pricing information? Did you see yourself using a clever ruse to embarrass or humiliate him?

Don't feel bad. I think that's a natural tendency, especially in an industry where we try our best to get the lowest prices, and subcontractors try their best to charge the highest prices. There is always a winner and a loser. You want to be the winner. I get that.

But still, please don't do it. Keep a good perspective.

The residential construction industry is small, and news travels fast. Bad news travels even faster. We homebuilders need subcontractors to build our houses. The days of us employing carpenters and masons are long past and not likely to ever return. In this story, the builder was as responsible for allowing prices to creep up as the subcontractor was in pushing them up.

After this episode, the relationship between this mason and me rose to an entirely different level. We were much closer and often talked about his relationships with his suppliers, even including his general liability insurance carriers—all in a collaborative way, so I could jump in to help him overcome obstacles where I could. We became a single team instead of competing teams, and that was worth more than any savings we could have achieved. It ensured sustainable savings because we were working together, on the same track instead of competing as passive aggressive rivals.

With this new story in mind, make a list of the subcontractors and material suppliers with whom you have the best rapport. They represent the construction categories that are likely the best place for you to start. Think of this exercise as a way to improve your overall teamwork by enveloping them as part of *your* team.

Now, for each of these categories, make a list of materials where it's important for you to identify unit pricing. You may want to include drywall, but not drywall screws and joint compound. You may wish to include masonry veneer, but not mortar and sealant. You may want to include roof tile and roofing paper, but not nails or flashings. You can decide what level of detail to start with and refine the process later as you become proficient in managing those costs. Likely, as you learn more about material and labor pricing, your curiosity alone will drive continual improvement.

I think the biggest mistake I made when starting this process was assuming that we, the homebuilder, were already doing everything well and had no room for improvement; therefore, the subcontractor had to make all the changes. Wow, was I wrong! Sometimes, I say dumb things. I'm trying to get better.

As I mentioned earlier, the best question I ever asked a subcontractor was, "What is it we do that costs you money?" The first time you ask, they will give you a safe, generic answer. As you keep asking and show you care (by making changes they suggest), you will start getting valuable information from them on how to lower their operating costs. Keep doing this, and your contract pricing will start creeping down for a change.

Imagine just by asking some questions you allowed them to see that their pricing practices were a bit too high. It goes a long way when you can show that your intent lies in not breaking them down but enlisting them in a new version of your team. Make them believe that is true through your actions.

Throughout my career in homebuilding, as we uncovered severe inefficiencies and pricing debacles, I often asked myself how we got here. Next, we'll explore something we are all responsible for doing—something that inadvertently has a negative impact on our industry—and how to correct it.

How We Got Here—Explained

Now that you've collaborated with your most trusted subcontractors and suppliers to establish unit pricing and accurate material quantities in your contracts, you are ready for the next level of integration with your new team members. Don't wait until all of your unit pricing tasks are complete to begin this stage; get started with the categories that you converted first.

Many years ago, in the earlier days of my role as purchasing manager, "George the Plumber" came into my office pleading with me *not* to add a new brand of faucets to our specifications. He explained how this change would cause him to carry a whole new inventory of products, which he did not have room for, as well as all the spare parts to service them.

He went on and on about how we were so intolerant of construction delays due to backorders, requiring him to keep sufficient inventory on hand of every faucet we specified. Because we also did not tolerate service calls after the homeowner moved in, sometimes spare parts were necessary to swap out the bad parts before move-in. He described the storage area of his warehouse and how there was just no room for another line of products, meaning he would have to lease more space to accommodate this change. I think he started talking about the extra costs . . . lamenting on and on.

Then without warning, sticking my hand in the air, I interrupted him, saying, "I don't care; just get it done." Seven little words that changed everything.

How did I get there? How did I arrive at such a perspective and attitude toward a guy like George? Here's the backstory.

In the late 1990s, we were the biggest homebuilder in San Diego, building 400 homes a year, on our way to 800 per year, without increasing staff. With my small department working on contracts for four new communities simultaneously, I could respond to only about one third of the emails I received each day. A never-ending stack of contract folders sat on my desk for my review while superintendents screamed for contracts to prevent construction delays. The pressure felt thick, unrelenting, and sticky.

We had just emerged from the recession of the early 1990s and were willing to do just about anything to sell a house. We began customizing homes, which then birthed the options program that allowed home buyers to personalize their home purchase through upgrade selections. Still, we remained hesitant to add to our staff, just in case these booming sales began to wane. Much was expected from every employee, and our sub-contractors found themselves in a similar state.

When George came in to voice his concern that our decisions were going to drive up costs, I wanted to care . . . I really did. But there was no time.

I can't forget the look on his face. I wish I could forget—that look of desperation, of last hope. Yet I was in survival mode, and what I needed most was to build houses fast. We were selling faster than we were building, with tons of pressure to increase building speed.

I wasn't the only one who was saying those seven little words. *I don't care; just get it done.* The whole industry was voicing them; we were all in the same boat. George came to me because . . . (and here's the saddest part) . . . he thought, of all the builders, I would be the one who would best understand his situation and the imminent cost implications. He trusted me.

And he left my office deeply disappointed.

As the years went by, I started to get an idea of how much money those seven little words cost us—cost our company, cost our industry. I am ashamed of myself for not taking the time to listen, really listen to George. He was telling me something monumentally important. Yet tasked with saving my company lots of money, I couldn't see the forest for the trees.

Here's the takeaway I learned that day with George: As a homebuilder, learn to focus on what you can do to lower the operating costs of your subcontractors and suppliers; learn from my mistake, and take those seven little words out of your company culture. The price is higher than you might imagine.

You can add all the faucet brands you want to your specifications. Just do it with the collaboration of your plumber so you fully understand the cost ramifications for both of you. Then, if you still decide to add them, you will be doing it with your eyes wide open. That's all I'm asking here.

The worst part of my *seven little words* episode is that, afterward, he stopped complaining about things we were doing that cost him money. I guess I assumed because he stopped complaining, we were doing better. We were not.

Your subcontractors and suppliers may be giving you hints that cost you money with operational decisions, and you don't even know it. Take a minute to think about what they have been telling you lately or used to tell you.

Knowing is half the battle. *Doing* is the other half.

Find out what you do that costs your subcontractors money, and then take action to correct this discrepancy. In most cases, it won't cost you any money, just a change in procedures, scheduling methods, or timely notifications. *This one thing you learn may be the most significant cost-saving action you ever take.*

In the next chapter, I'll present you with a cost-saving supply chain solution so simple you may laugh. Then, you'll wonder why we didn't do it forty years ago.

FINAL THOUGHTS: FROM BIG FISH TO SMALL FISH, ALL IN ONE MEETING

Before we, the six regional supply chain VPs, unbundled our labor and materials costs, we thought we were doing pretty well. Until we met our new boss. There we were sitting around a conference table at the home office, often referred to as the Mothership, waiting to meet him. Jerry entered the room like the Tasmanian devil, vigorously proclaiming he was going to show us how to create supply contracts like we'd never seen before. He was excited, to say the least.

With no time to waste, he asked which construction category we should start with. We were still stunned by his burst of energy and ambition. He said, "How about drywall?" adding, "What difference does it make where we start? We're going to do them all anyway."

We didn't even know what he was talking about yet, so we agreed, "Let's start with drywall," shrugging our shoulders.

He said, "Okay, we're going to have negotiations with drywall manufacturers and distributors like never before. We'll start making our own drywall if we have to. But first things, first. I need to know what kind of volume we're talking about."

Still standing, his hand ready to write a number on the whiteboard, he asked, "How many sheets of drywall are we currently buying?" The room was silent. "Come on, guys, I need to know how much drywall we buy each year so I can use that as leverage in my negotiations. How much drywall do we buy?"

The room still sat silent as we all squirmed uncomfortably in our chairs.

I can't remember who spoke up first; it wasn't me. But someone told him we only buy directly in one or two locations, and the rest of our markets are turn-key[13], lump-sum contracts, *so we aren't really sure how much drywall we buy.* This same VP quickly added that we could come up with an average per house and multiply that by the number of homes we build to arrive at a ballpark quantity.

Jerry stood dumbfounded. "You mean to tell me we build 40,000 homes per year, and we don't know how much drywall we buy?"

We sheepishly nodded.

Jerry paused. We had just taken a large chunk of wind out of his sails. This was going to be more difficult than he thought.

"Okay," he reasoned, "we can work with an average multiplied by 40,000 . . . I can work with that. Okay, let's move on." With his face turned toward the whiteboard, pen in hand, ready to write, he asked, "How much do we currently pay for a sheet of drywall?" Silence.

Jerry, with the look of shock and dismay on his face, the wind completely knocked out of his sails, asked a clarifying question just to see if he'd gotten this right. "We build 40,000 homes per year, have been building houses for over forty years, and we don't know how many sheets of drywall we buy or how much we pay for a sheet of drywall. Did I get that right?"

---

[13] *Turn-key* is a term indicating that all labor and materials needed to complete the task are included. This relieves that builder from having to call out every part and every step in the process of a subcontractor's portion of building a house.

The look in our eyes was answer enough. The face of embarrassment isn't pretty.

Jerry put the cap on the whiteboard marker and threw it. Hands on his hips, he resounded, "We have a lot of work to do before I can even get started with what I was hired for." That was the beginning of a difficult two-day meeting in a conference room at the Mothership, which we all thought we might have to rename the Death Star.

Until that day, we considered ourselves one of the nation's highest performing home-building companies. We touted the highest scores in customer satisfaction, multiple awards as one of the best places to work, and one of the most profitable homebuilders. In our eyes, we sat on top of the world.

Jerry gave us a new perspective. In the following months we worked around the clock to get all our contracts converted to unit-price agreements with correct quantities and ultimately gave Jerry what he needed to do his magic. At that time in the industry, we were all struggling to get houses built fast enough, so our focus shifted from primarily cost-savings to a production capacity initiative, with cost reduction secondary. Ultimately, we got the houses built, and we saved a boatload of money at the same time.

If all we had accomplished was saving a bunch of money and getting preferential treatment from material suppliers and subcontractors that enabled getting all our houses built, we would have considered it an enormous success. We got so much more.

We had a paradigm shift in how we viewed the interaction of homebuilders, subcontractors, distributors, and manufacturers. We previously thought that our supplier relations had to be adversarial, and our suppliers did, too. We were wrong.

We thought, without ever asking, that subcontractors would never give us unit pricing. We were wrong.

We thought getting volume rebates from manufacturers was the most we could get from that relationship. We were wrong.

I have a friend who races canoes in Hawaii, and I've been in the water with him a few times. Each time, he strives to get us to work together as a team, pulling synchronously to the sound of his commanding cadence. It's a lot of work to paddle a canoe. He does it in races from Oahu to Maui and back, an 80-mile race.

The last time I was with him, we just paddled around the bay and exhausted ourselves, approaching the point of complete muscle failure. Then, suddenly we felt it. The point when everyone begins pulling at precisely the same time, and the canoe suddenly becomes slippery in the water, our speed increasing dramatically.

Then, as quickly as it came, when one person got out of sync, we slowed down again, even though we were still paddling as hard as we could. Yet we knew not to stop there; we knew to try to sync up again.

For all canoers it's a continuous struggle, and the team that perseveres and stays in sync the longest wins the race.

I was headed back to the airport after two days of meetings at the Mothership, thinking about what we discussed and where we were about to go. I knew that home-building would never be the same again, and for some reason, I was happy about it. I truly believed that we were going to learn how to be slippery in the water and achieve lower costs while increasing the production capacity of our subcontractors and suppliers. I couldn't wait to get started.

PART II

The Methodology

CHAPTER 3

Last Mile Logistics

P arker brought his lawn chair and wide-brimmed hat to the job site, sat down, got comfortable, and watched. He was a supply chain manager from another industry, a fresh set of eyes to help us identify opportunities for improvement. We sent him out there to watch the painters, to count how many gallons of paint were brought to the site and how many were used to cover the house. He sat there all day long for three days observing the painting operation in several homes. While he sat there, he noticed some other things, too.

Parker called me on the phone and asked a single question—a novel question, one I don't remember having ever been asked. As I started to answer in the way any veteran construction person would do, I began to question my own response. *Was I really answering what he was asking*? Still, I gave him my thoughts anyway.

Parker's question was simple: "Why are there always two-and-a-half truckloads of drywall coming to the site?"

I fired off my response quickly, saying something like, "The amount of drywall being delivered is just enough for the two houses ready to stock drywall in them. If any additional drywall were brought to the site, it would have to be stored somewhere and then moved to the appropriate house when ready, causing that portion of drywall to be moved twice, not just once. So this is the most efficient method."

But Parker was one step ahead of me. He had already thought of this reason and countered with an astute observation. "Since the next house in the sequence is almost ready," he asked, "could they not have put more drywall on the truck and stocked the second floor of the next house?" Then he continued, "If half a house is ready, and the truck is coming to the site anyway, why would they not fill the truck *full* of drywall?"

Ready with another quick response, I stated that the drywall payment structure was based on a whole house of drywall, while a house only half delivered could not be invoiced. Parker said, "So? The remaining drywall would be delivered in a few days, qualifying that house for payment on the same monthly invoice."

I began to feel woefully unqualified to answer Parker's simple questions. And his next question cemented that notion.

"Can we put something else on the half-full truck, like floor tile or light fixtures or toilets?" he asked.

You see, Parker saw this as a missed opportunity. In his experience with supply chain management, every square inch on a truck is valuable space. Once a truck starts down the road, you have the same logistics cost, whether it's full, half-full, or has just one box sitting on it.

So if not drywall, could we add another item to the half-full truck? This time, fighting the temptation to blurt out one of my clever responses, I thought about it. For a long time.

Why not, indeed?

And in that moment I understood his perspective, how it was different from my own, and how it contrasted with the traditional methods of building production houses. He had no idea how his question rocked the foundation of a seventy-year tradition of how to deliver construction materials to a job site.

It was this new understanding that forms the basis for this chapter. We will explore three unique examples, introducing you to the subcontractors and material suppliers that helped make this an industry-first transformation of last-mile logistics consolidation.

LOOKING IN FROM THE OUTSIDE

It may sound surprising that a revelation that found its way into this book was inspired by someone outside our industry. Who sat in a lawn chair. On a construction site. For three days. Plus, his question was so innocent, so simple, I almost bulldozed over it with my forty years of experience—without really considering what he said. One more ounce of pride and arrogance on my part and this cost-saving jewel could have been lost forever.

Because this story speaks to the perspective of someone from the outside looking in, who asked simple questions, which can lead to reducing the cost of building a home, it has intriguing value.

We, as homebuilders, often tell ourselves that we are doing everything we can to keep costs down. We say it all the time. I think it may be more accurate, though, if we say we are doing everything *we know how* to keep costs down. We should stay open to new ideas, no matter how crazy they may seem. As you are about to see, every person involved in this exercise initially thought we were crazy.

If our aim is to lower the price of a home so more people can buy houses, we should remain open to new ways to lower the cost of our construction processes. Doesn't it make sense that reducing the cost to deliver materials to the house could be one of the contributing elements of lowering total costs? Why, then, had I never, in all my years of experience, considered making an effort to control my construction costs by controlling the cost of getting the materials to the job site? What prevented me from arriving at this idea on my own? It turns out I am as much a victim of tradition as anyone else, it pains me to say. As trucking costs rise, those increases apply equally to half-full trucks as well as to full ones.

I think it's fair to assume that the subcontractors and material distributors are doing their very best. After all, they are the industry experts of their particular construction category; inevitably, their core competencies include finding the most effective way to get materials to the job site. And I think it's true: They do prove effective, from a certain point of view.

The HVAC subcontractor, for example, manages material deliveries as efficiently as possible within the HVAC category. We don't fault him for not collaborating with the electrician and the plumber to have one distributor bring all their finish products[14] together on the same truck, even though all those materials get delivered and installed on the same day.

Our expectations of subcontractors managing materials have, up to this point, been limited to the materials they install. Homebuilders contract separately with each subcontractor, rarely blending responsibilities between multiple companies. How, then, will we ever realize significantly lower logistics costs? Can we continue to tell ourselves we are doing everything possible to control costs, knowing that we haven't even delved

---

[14] HVAC *finish products* include thermostats, air registers, and grilles. *Electrical finish products* include switches, receptacles, light fixtures, and bulbs. Plumbing finish products include toilets, sinks, faucets, drain covers, shower handles, and heads.

into an exploration of more effective ways to carry materials to the site?

Next, we will explore a new perspective on material management that makes finding efficiency opportunities fun and easy. Well, fun, for certain.

LESS TIRE TRACKS

Materials are delivered to the job site on large flatbed trucks, small flatbed trucks, trucks with crane arms, pick-up trucks, and the occasional 1991 Oldsmobile Cutlass Supreme. The subcontractors, not the builder, arrange these deliveries. These subcontractors have a tremendous amount of experience, having done this for decades. Why, then, haven't any of them thought to put door hardware and light fixtures on the same truck and reduce delivery costs by 50 percent in an instant?

Subcontractors are not to blame. Our subcontract agreements are structured to confine the management of materials to each subcontractor's category only. They spend years cultivating relationships with manufacturers and distributors, continually searching for the lowest prices, including the cost of hauling material to the site. Part of their strategy includes delaying payment as long as possible. Once materials are ordered, the subcontractor forfeits his opportunity to switch suppliers if he finds a lower price. So they have learned not to order materials until twenty-four to forty-eight hours before they need them. The longer they can float invoices, meaning order products without yet paying for them, the more cash flow is available to run their business. And if the builder pays the subcontractor fast, he may even get paid before he has to pay the supplier.

This delay in ordering materials just a few days in advance creates challenges for the distributor. With only one or two days to fill an order, not enough time is left for any kind of optimization. It's barely enough time to fill the order and find a way to get it delivered on time.

Many distributors have their own trucks, and when they have time to optimize deliveries, they can ensure full trucks leave the yard and follow a carefully mapped-out route that minimizes the delivery time and mileage. Yet when urgency belies their only planning method, trucks are less full than they should be. Trucking costs, whether outsourced or under a supplier's ownership, have been rising steadily since 2012 with no ceiling in sight. Logistics consume a much greater portion of our construction costs than before, making it even more deserving of our attention.

Last-mile logistics prove particularly costly. Where long-haul trucks can keep their cost per mile down by covering long distances quickly on freeways, last-mile deliveries navigate the city or rural roads, go out full (ideally), come back empty, and seek job sites not yet on maps. If we use $300 as an average cost for each last-mile delivery on a construction site, and each house gets about thirty-five deliveries, this equates to a total last-mile logistics cost of $10,500. Savings of merely 20 percent can reduce material costs by $2,100 per house. Worth trying? I think so.

First, we have to change the perspective of whoever is managing logistics. When the focus is shifted from the management of one category to all categories, Parker's question about putting something else on the back of that half-empty drywall truck doesn't seem so wild. This shift in perspective is the single most crucial component of being successful in optimizing homebuilding logistics. Think about who is managing the logistics for your homebuilding operations today. Are they doing a good job?

Once I learned to view last-mile logistics differently, it became difficult to ignore the opportunity to reduce costs by managing them jointly. Or just managing them at all. Most builders have no focus on logistics; they just let it happen as it does, hoping for the best. The information in this chapter will help you establish a strategy that is more effective, more grounded, and more sustainable than simple wishful thinking.

And that's what I discovered through ideas and solutions such as the ones Parker imparted to me. Parker and I worked together for a couple of years; he taught me supply chain management, and I taught him construction. Because of him, I learned to look at job site logistics with a new perspective, and together we came up with some great ways to save money. All of them simple, but none of them easy to implement, at least as the first builder to put them in action.

This work entailed us questioning every delivery, interviewing the subcontractors that ordered the materials, and engaging in discussions with the distributors who brought them to the site. Each subcontractor had a good reason for doing what they were doing, but none of them could answer if it were possible to combine materials on one truck. They had never considered it. The most common answer was, "I suppose so, I think . . . wait a minute."

I mentioned earlier that homebuilders celebrate when they can find a $50 savings. Imagine what happens when you find thousands of dollars by optimizing logistics. No amount of brainstorming in a conference room could have validated such a claim or justified the efforts required to transform a process cemented in decades of tradition.

When we reduce the number of delivery trucks, we reduce the cost of materials. I admit, the significance behind this sentence is painfully obvious, but why then has our industry not taken this point more seriously? Why had I, a self-proclaimed industry expert, not figured it out on my own? It took Parker sitting in a lawn chair for three days and asking the right questions for me to get it.

In the next three sections, I'll give you details on how you can implement a reduction in logistics costs yourself. What I want you to take away from these examples is the understanding that you can optimize logistics in an infinite number of ways to fit any circumstance. All you need to get started are a new perspective and an open mind.

On the Back of the Truck

Parker and I met with the owner and general manager (GM) of the drywall distributor, gigantic smiles on our faces, eager to present our great idea. They were going to love it, and we would walk out as heroes who saved the day, increasing revenue to the drywall distributor and reducing costs to us. Win-win. We couldn't wait to see the look on their faces. When was the last time a builder did something like this for them, huh? This was probably the first time. We were so excited.

We sat down in the conference room of this successful, privately-owned drywall distribution company. They had been in business for over twenty years and had nine locations, and we were sitting in their largest branch, the only one with a conference room. We sat down, opened our folders, displayed the spreadsheets and charts we had prepared, and stated the case for having them put ceramic floor tile on the back of their drywall trucks. After a long, detailed presentation, laying it all out, we leaned back, smiled at each other, and waited for the accolades to begin.

They looked at each other, looked at us, looked at each other again, looked at us, and in unison said, "No."

Our detailed proposal included renting a small area of their warehouse to store a buffer of floor tile, not too much. I think we started with about fifteen square yards and offered a fair price per square yard. The buffer acted as a cushion for when the construction schedule fluctuated, allowing for a continual flow of materials to the site when ordering another full truck from the tile manufacturer was not feasible, plus it relieved some anxiety for those nervous about this new process. Over time, and as we all became confident in the new process, buffer inventory would be reduced to about a three-week supply. We used historical data to decide which colors to stock. The drywall distributors were already in the business of forklifting materials onto a truck at their warehouse/yard and then using the piggy-back forklifts on the back of the truck to offload at the job site. The only change for them was the material on the pallet and an additional manufacturer to receive materials from.

Concerns about the construction schedule's capacity to direct a drywall delivery to one house and a ceramic tile delivery to another, without the ceramic tile arriving too late or too early, were quickly alleviated. We found an ideal rhythm after just a few weeks of executing this process. The high-velocity community where we piloted this process allowed us to see proof of concept quickly. The test scenario succeeded with flying colors, and while I admit this process would be challenging to implement in some communities, it worked great in most places. In the end, the drywall distributor's revenue would increase with just a minor increase in additional cost (a few more minutes for the forklift driver), and the ceramic tile manufacturer benefited from our quick-pay system, something they welcomed with open arms. Truly a win-win-win.

So with all this testing history already in the books, the emphatic "no" from the drywall distributor that day left us momentarily paralyzed. Yet, still confident in the value of our proposal, we knew we just needed to present the information differently. We decided to give them some time, so we asked them to think about it and scheduled another meeting for the following week. We rationalized that they initially said "no" because we were asking them to do something far outside their comfort zone. They knew nothing about floor tile or the manufacturer who provided it. So saying "no" was the easiest response.

Parker and I had been working on this strategy presentation for a week, giving our continual, undivided attention to the vetting of every angle of this deal. By the time we presented it to the drywall guys, we had already drunk from the firehose and were full. We should have considered the shock effect the proposal might have had on them and eased our way into it a bit slower.

In total, we met with them six times before they agreed to our proposal. We did not attempt to convince or coerce them in any way; we just kept answering their questions and offering insights we thought were relevant. In the end, they talked themselves into proceeding.

Going through this process "brought about a new level of self-awareness to what kind of a company we are," they admitted. "We're a bulk distributor. If you need a forklift to put it on the truck and a forklift to unload it, that's the business we're good at. It doesn't really matter what's on the pallet." Their business turned a corner that day.

A high-velocity production homebuilding operation. That's how I would describe the community where we began this process: It started four homes and finished four homes each day, with a sixty-eight-day construction cycle time. The home buyers in this community had a choice of only four colors for the floor tile area. This high-velocity community with a limited number of tile SKUs enabled a quick success for the drywall distributor—and for us. Our net savings with this one strategy was $85 per house. Once set up, it required little effort on our part to keep it going.

This illustrates how job by job, or market by market, differing circumstances can enable or disable individual supply chain solutions. Combining floor tile and drywall on the same truck worked great at this particular community. While $85 per house may not sound like much, it gave us the practice we needed to apply the same principle to other materials that netted more substantial savings. A little here, a little there, it all adds up.

I have learned that skilled material management is not a core competency of most subcontractors. More of a necessary evil, I'd say, as they do their best not to lose money doing it. By taking the ceramic tile out of the subcontractor's contract, we relieved him of the burden of managing the physical material, allowing him to focus on his real core competency: installing flooring materials. Now he had more available credit and capital to do other things, which contributed to increasing his production capacity—so vital to construction operations in a tight labor market.

Our drywall distributor recognized something new about themselves as they changed their future business strategies and enabled substantial growth—a satisfying result that eluded them before. Don't let "because that's the way we've always done it" prevent you from transforming last-mile logistics and seeing a decrease in building material costs. The effects of helping a company improve its business operations often result in lower prices for you, giving you an even bigger advantage. The best thing about this deal? You now have friends in the drywall business that will never forget what you did for them.

Before we move on to the next section, I want you to think about a list of materials you might be able to consolidate onto one truck in your area. I suspect that while you were reading this section, some material categories came to mind. Don't filter what pops into your head with the conventional wisdom of past operations; just write them all down and then collaborate with suppliers and subcontractors to generate ideas on how it could work.

Next, we'll explore another last-mile logistics consolidation approach that is similar to this story but with a surprising twist.

SCOOP THEM BACK IN THE BOX

Lightning Wholesale is an excellent electrical distributor. They not only supply our subcontractors with an assortment of electrical wiring materials, the light fixtures we purchase from them directly are always all kitted up into one or two boxes and delivered to the job site for our electrician to install. Over the many years we worked with Lightning, they rarely made a mistake. We were impressed with their high level of customer service, attention to detail, flexibility with last-minute changes, and perseverance to continually improve.

So we felt sure about them, confident, like we could count on them to always have our back. We were so confident that when we approached them about combining door hardware and light fixtures on the same delivery truck (in a typical construction schedule, those two products go to the same house on the same day), they were going to love and champion the idea. We sat down with the owner and GM in a small conference room in the corporate office location inside one of their largest stores. We were a fast-paying customer, and they were happy to welcome us in. They said that, in fifty years, this was the first time a production homebuilder came to their office. Light refreshments were even brought in for the special occasion, something they rarely did.

Feeling happy and hopeful, we laid our plan out in detail. From our last experience, we had learned that our proposal needed to paint a clear picture of how this would work and what was in it for them. Proud of this presentation and anticipating the accolades it would receive, we finally put the pinnacle question in front of them: "Will you agree to receive door hardware from our manufacturer, who will be paid by us, and deliver it together with light fixtures on the same truck?"

A flat-out "no" rang in our ears.

Well, they probably said "no" with a bit more diplomacy than how we heard it, but the answer was no just the same. Having heard this response before, we knew we just had to ask it differently.

We did, and again they said "no."

When we started to reframe the question a third time, they politely interrupted us, stating they were an electrical distributor, had been in business for over fifty years, had twenty-three locations, and their people were electrical experts. They didn't know anything about door hardware. "If a box of locks were to fall off the table and door hardware fell out," they said, "our people wouldn't know what to do with it. They don't know anything about locks."

We left Lightning's office with the agreement that they would think about it, and we would meet again the next week to hear their thoughts. Parker and I left the office with our heads hanging low. We were sure we had the right proposal and presentation this time. We kept asking ourselves, *what did we do wrong?*

We met with Lightning's team seven more times. Each time, we left with the potential of a deal hanging by a thread. We spent time with their front-line employees, with their department managers, and in their packing and staging areas, role-playing how they would manage the "box of locks." Finally, one of their managers, Joe, said he could do it, and we all agreed to try it on a short-term basis. *It's better than nothing*, I thought.

Joe spent much of his time visualizing how to make this work. His team used empty boxes to mock the box of locks and practiced receiving, staging, and shipping the locks with the light fixtures. We visited them once more just before the go-live date, just to see how things were going. And an amazing thing happened. They had come to the self-realization that *what we do well is move cartons. If it comes in a cardboard box, we are good at receiving, storing, staging, and delivering those boxes. It doesn't really matter that much what's in the box.* They decided that if the box fell over and locks came out, they would simply scoop them back in and tape the box. I was so proud of them.

In no time, Lightning Wholesale was operating the most efficient door hardware last-mile logistics model that homebuilding had ever seen. We paid them a small fee to store a buffer amount of material in their warehouse, a small fee to receive products from the manufacturer, and a small fee to send them to the job site: a total of about $19 per house. When you simply receive a package in one door and send it out the other door, it's called cross-docking. Lightning Wholesale discovered they were very good at cross-docking. After deducting the door hardware materials from our subcontractor's turn-key contract and paying Lightning for their new services, we netted a $135 savings per house.

In case something went wrong, we staged a safety stock of door hardware on the job sites just to mitigate a potential disruption to the installer. This was a step demanded by the installer, construction superintendents, our operations VP, and Lightning Wholesale. In the end, we never used any of the safety stock. The subcontractor later confessed he did not believe we could figure out in three months what took him sixteen years to perfect: getting the *right materials* in the *right place* at the *right time*—every time. We organized this project, but the manufacturer—who created a box of locks specific to each address—did all the work effortlessly, combined with Lightning Wholesale's cross-docking skills. Once we set this up, it ran flawlessly, requiring no effort or maintenance from us.

With this new example in mind, which construction material categories would you consider for consolidation? Look at your list, identify the categories that exemplify your best supplier relations, and start brainstorming with them. You can consolidate distribution with just about any supplier, but we found it immensely helpful to work with suppliers with whom we had already built mutual trust. We found trust to be one of the most important elements in successfully consolidating distribution.

Looking back, we could have easily taken "no" for an answer and gone back to our office, testifying that last-mile logistics consolidation fails to work in our industry with no questions asked. But if we had, at least two companies would have missed out on knowing and utilizing the skills they were truly good at, and we would have continued losing out on opportunities to innovate the supply chain.

Certainly, in some of our discussions with suppliers, I seemed to hone my knack of agitating pain points they didn't know they had. Yet thankfully, with the mutual trust and respect we had built, our conversations ended in a $135 per house savings instead of an argument. Because the realization that they could use their newly recognized skills and reap tremendous savings proved such an epiphany for Lightning Wholesale, something for which the owner is eternally grateful, I counted it as one of the more gratifying things I had accomplished as a builder, partially because of its uniqueness.

I'll always remember the terrific feeling of helping others in the supply chain to grow and excel while at the same time accomplishing a tremendous goal for our own company, a feeling I hope others in this industry can experience as well as they strive for relationships and opportunities to mutually benefit one another.

The bottom line is all about *continual improvement.* If you have the right foundational strategy, a sound continual improvement process can produce an effective way to continually reduce costs. When you can achieve your business goals by lowering other people's costs and not just unilaterally take the profit out of your subcontractor's pockets, the savings become sustainable and improvable.

Next, we will explore a consolidation strategy in which we can partially attribute a cost savings to merely gaining visibility in the area of *how much is the milk?*

What Else Can We Put Back There?

Four of our children are boys. And as an astute parent over the years, my wife has coined the term "two boys are dumber than one." Of course, I informed her that when boys get together, not all their ideas are bad. I'm relatively sure that's a factual statement. Take, for example, what happened when Parker and I came up with an idea on how to expand the process of putting something else on the back of a drywall delivery truck. If we could put the floor tile on the truck and save money, we wondered *what else can we put back there?*

Seeking answers to this question illustrates the natural progression of one of our goals. One of our top goals focused on this: How can we gain visibility into how much we're paying for materials and their quantities? Well, when you put your heads together, you simply get ideas.

Unit price visibility opens the gateway to a whole new world of creative visualization that defies the traditions of conventional construction operations. And here's the key: It's not something you have to direct your people to do. It happens naturally, and when they start to see layers of mystery pulled back, curiosity advances the process.

Previously, we had made a private label deal with a stucco manufacturer and a direct buying deal with a stucco lath and building paper manufacturer. Our new idea was to combine all these and have the drywall distributor deliver both drywall and stucco materials, reducing the number of trucks bringing the same amount of building materials.

We had already paid for the drywall delivery truck when we purchased the drywall. So, we reasoned, anything else we put into an otherwise empty part of a truck gets a free ride to the job site. We just had to pay the drywall distributor a small fee to receive, load, and unload these new materials—entailing a minimal price.

This example of last-mile logistics consolidation, combined with the others I've cited, hardly offers a definitive list of opportunities. But you can draw on infinite combinations of materials, applying them to all your associated distributors and manufacturers, to create efficiencies that work great for you. If nothing else, I hope this stimulates your ideas of the many real possibilities, motivating you to start down this path.

Despite our experience of adding floor tile to the back of a drywall truck, our new idea still met with reluctance. Yet just like in the last two examples, after several meetings, all parties agreed. From then on, I think the drywall guys winced a bit whenever I came walking through their door . . . and breathed sighs of relief when I said my goodbyes.

Kidding aside, I believe we positively influenced their business improvements, which they said they would never forget.

The drywall distributor's revenue increased through the fees they garnered from carrying more products—now efficiently filling trucks while adding only small operating costs for loading a few more pallets. The dream of every business lies in increasing revenue while adding minimal additional cost, thus increasing their profit margins. This drywall distributor had all that to celebrate—a "yay!" moment for each of us.

The stucco manufacturer gained more business through the private label program, guaranteeing to gain 100 percent of our business. The small act of using a different bag while filling it with stucco brought nearly no extra cost, increasing their revenue without increasing their expenditures. Similar benefits were realized by the lath wire and paper manufacturers, who often get shopped by subcontractors who are always looking for a product that is a penny cheaper somewhere else.

After we knew all our suppliers were reaping higher revenue, we sat down and tallied what benefits we had received. In total, this project netted a $1,300 per house cost savings for us.

Once in place, this process worked flawlessly, with not even a bit of maintenance on our part. It makes you wonder why anyone hadn't done this before. Why didn't our subcontractors? Why didn't we? In the grand scheme of things, logistics is a pretty small piece of the pie. Builders don't need to buy every material for a house like we did in the 1970s; we just need to use existing resources more efficiently. Subcontractors will only concern themselves with the materials necessary to support their installations, nothing more. Without the builder taking the lead on initiatives like this, it would never get done. Solutions like this require a whole-house perspective.

Before reading these examples, you might have dismissed any suggestion of working on last-mile logistics consolidation because you may not have known the possibilities. I'd like you to envision the short- and long-term benefits of controlling cost through optimization of logistics, having fewer trucks bringing the same amount of materials to your job sites.

Now that you have visualized your operations in a new light, write down your fresh, even unprecedented ideas. Write them all down; you can dismiss bad ideas later. For now, capture all your thoughts on paper. You might balk at the idea of putting a lawn chair on a job site and sitting there observing for a few days, but that exercise gained us, in total, about ten times Parker's annual salary. I highly recommend trying it.

At a time when prices are rising due to high demand or not going down fast enough when the housing market shrinks, it helps to have more control of your costs. Logistics gives you just one of the many ways to do so, and like the other methods discussed in this book, it starts with unit-price contracts. In times of high demand, when resources are stretched and builders struggle to build houses on time partly due to subcontractors' production capacity constraints, that's when logistics solutions like these can provide some relief to an already over-stretched subcontractor.

In the next chapter, I'll demonstrate other opportunities to control costs, specifically when production homebuilders buy materials, either directly from a manufacturer or a distributor, and discover how to manage these materials with the least amount of effort and risk. I don't recommend that builders buy all their materials directly, as we did in the 1970s, but I think buying specific ones directly can offer key advantages.

FINAL THOUGHTS: PUSHING TASKS UP THE CHAIN

One Monday morning at our operations meeting, it was my week to report on our supply chain pilot programs. With my first full report in hand after beginning some of our pilots, I'm sure the sales and marketing departments didn't want to hear it, much less be there. Perhaps everyone held the same sentiments: low expectations. Until now, all they had heard from my department was *costs are going up . . . again.*

On the prior Friday evening, most people had already gone home, but I was still there, putting the finishing touches on the presentation needed for Monday. I was to report on the progress of our supply chain solutions to my colleagues, who were skeptical every step of the way, questioning and sometimes scoffing at some of my pilot programs. Some believers would sit amidst the gathering, I was sure, but they wouldn't show their hand in meetings with their peers. I didn't mind; I knew they simply *didn't know what they didn't know* and considered it my job to show them how beneficial these strategies could be.

Then Monday arrived, and slide after slide, I presented a compilation of each pilot program, showing the tasking of subcontractors, distributors, manufacturers, and construction superintendents alongside the savings achieved. As each slide advanced, jaws fell closer to the floor. Nobody expected we could save so much money without going out to bid again. As I finished and sat down, the operations team did not want it to end; they asked me questions for another half hour or so. They sat amazed. Suddenly, they had discovered a whole new world of supply chain management they didn't know existed.

An incremental degradation of sophistication advances as you move down the supply chain—from manufacturers, to distributors, to dealers, to subcontractors.

Manufacturers practice continual improvement strategies such as kaizen and kanban, using statistical process controls and the latest software to support continual incremental improvements.

In contrast, subcontractors deliver materials to the job site in a 1991 Oldsmobile Cutlass Supreme (have I mentioned that before?). I don't mean to speak ill of our subcontractors. They do a great job of building our homes, but for many of them, their core competency is not material management; it's installing construction materials—and building houses.

I have discovered that, for most situations and supplies, the further up the supply chain you push a material-related activity, the more likely the task will be done more efficiently and at lower cost.

Some communities provide opportunities that others do not, just as some homebuilders have capabilities that others don't. There is no one-size-fits-all supply chain strategy for our industry. This applies to buying lumber just as well as buying door hardware or windows. You have to create the strategies that work best for you and your supply chain partners. Before you can do so, however, *you need to know who your supply chain partners are.*

Okay, this phrase may sound silly. Certainly, we know this, right? Well, I have learned that most of us don't know where the milk is coming from, so to speak. In most cases, we only see that we awarded a turn-key, lump-sum contract to a subcontractor, and he procures materials from . . . somewhere. Homebuilders typically do not know who their subcontractors are buying from and, therefore, remain ill-equipped to create supply chain strategies that can improve costs and operational efficiencies.

Despite my years of experience, even I was surprised who some of my supply chain companies were and how involved, or uninvolved, they were in my construction operations. Chances are, you will be surprised at some of the players in your supply chain, too. But knowing exactly who they are stands vital to reducing construction costs.

In the conference room that Monday morning, a spontaneous applause erupted. It may actually have been the first, but that response is far from typical. Soon after I walked out of that meeting, I felt energized, ready to amp up my game. The emotional strength gained from their consummate approval gave me fresh, new armor to take on a whole new set of naysayers, obstacles, and rejections. I was ready.

But believe me, the strongholds torn down and doors that swung open were not just surprising. They took some scrappy maneuvering and agile footwork, but in the end, we saw victory in ways that you can, too.

CHAPTER 4

Builder-Supplied Materials

One day in the conference room of the corporate office, I sat alone, waiting for the next bidder to arrive. Entertaining bidders for national contracts was usually more than a one-person show, but as the door hardware category was small, I was asked to do this one on my own. By *small*, I mean relative to how much we spend on it each year compared to other categories, and besides, there were only two bidders. I could easily handle this.

I had met with the first bidder earlier that day, hearing them pitch their proposition to me in its brightest light. They were hoping to be selected as our single-source supplier for the next three years. Just as I expected, the first presentation ended without a single surprise, and I anticipated the second one to promise much of the same, with only a brand name to differentiate the two. Selecting one over the other would simply be a function of the lowest price. Easy-peasy.

This second presentation started just like the first, and I sat up, trying to appear as attentive as the occasion demanded. Then I saw something that made me sit up a little taller, suddenly pushing me to the edge of my seat. I temporarily slipped into a mild state of shock over what I saw—a first for our industry and, indeed, for the door hardware product category.

Door hardware typically doesn't change much; this was before WiFi-enabled locks, so setting themselves apart proved challenging, especially when bidding on a substantial three-year contract for 100 percent exclusivity with one of the nation's top five homebuilding companies. The process was agonizing, and I felt for them. I don't even know what I would have done if I were sitting on their side of the table. Door hardware just doesn't give you much to work with; it's door hardware.

The brilliance of their proposal's new aspect lay in their innovative way to meet a need that we indeed had but didn't articulate very well in our Request for Proposal (RFP).[15] Our tepid communication about one of our pain points did not warrant the response they brought to the table. The ability to recognize this need was praiseworthy by itself.

This meeting occurred during a time when home sales had climbed so high we could barely build houses on time with the labor and materials available to us. That's why I included a section in the RFP that required the manufacturer to guarantee to supply us with adequate materials, preventing construction delays to any of our communities—and giving us preferential treatment over their other customers to do so. At the time I wrote

---

[15] Buyers issue a *Request for Proposal*, soliciting the seller's solution and price based on project specifications. A Request for Quote (RFQ) is similar but only asks for a price, not necessarily a solution, on what is specifically stated in the RFQ. Homebuilders generally issue RFPs for labor and material subcontracts and RFQs for materials only.

that RFP section, it was all I thought I could expect from a door hardware manufacturer. Certainly, the first bidder covered this request in their presentation, stating they would do just that. But the second bidder went far beyond.

The second bidder laid out a process that would not only supply us with an adequate supply of locks but would also increase the production capacity of the subcontractors installing them. Yes, we were in desperate need of these benefits. They proposed to put all the doorknobs and locks required for a particular house into a single box and ship it to our choice of locations. Ship it to our installer's shop, ship it to the house under construction, or ship it to a distributor already bringing other things to the house, like light fixtures, for example. Mind-blowing.

Typically, a door hardware manufacturer sells truckload quantities to a distributor, who sells pallet quantities to a dealer, who sells case quantities to a subcontractor. If the subcontractor has a large enough operation, he may buy pallet loads of products from a distributor and store them in his warehouse with a crew dedicated to picking and packing all the doorknobs and locks required for a particular house, a process commonly referred to as "Pick 'n Pack." The installer then stops by the shop before going to the job site and picks up his packaged locks, often kept in a yard-waste trash bag labeled for a particular house.

So travel with me back to the conference room that day. The second bidder had heard our nearly silent plea for help with production capacity without us ever making a loud or blatant request. I was so impressed that they recognized this, I stayed on the edge of my seat until the rest of the meeting was over.

In the chair I was occupying, you're supposed to keep a poker face, not allowing the bidder to know they have an advantage, thus compelling them to keep adding more to the pot. Typically, I'm quite good at it. Not this day.

The astute idea of packing these locks at the manufacturing plant relieves some steps in the supply chain, a benefit for sure, but more importantly, it alleviates many of the subcontractor's tasks in areas like subcontractor inventory, Pick 'n Pack detail, procurement, accounts payable, cash output, and the installer's extra trip to the shop to pick up the locks. It really does help increase a subcontractor's production capacity. Maybe not so much when their services are in low demand, but when they are stretched as tight as a rubber band about to snap, these areas loom large.

In the meeting, the instant this door hardware supplier put up on the screen that box of locks packed at the plant, I knew what that meant to the whole supply chain and to my installers. My prior experience in exploring various supply chain solutions prepared me for this moment. Although they were ready to spell it out for me, I didn't need it. I was finishing their sentences at this portion of the presentation—another thing a good poker player never does. I couldn't help it. I was witnessing a hinge point that this category of products had never seen.

This strategic sourcing deal captured a little over $4,000,000 over the duration of that contract. We would have considered that alone a big win, accolades all around. That much in cost savings for such a small construction category is generally unheard of. In this case, though, it ended up being the tip of the iceberg. This new awareness of possibilities discovered from a box of locks forms the basis of this chapter. Here I will explore several specific examples with you, illustrating the successes and struggles—as well as direct and indirect monetary benefits—of procuring your own building materials.

To Buy or Not to Buy?

Because I had already invested so much time over the years following the flow of building materials throughout the home-building supply chain, I was qualified to recognize the tremendous opportunity presented to us by the second bidder that day. Most people in a similar position are merely looking for a manufacturer's rebate, nothing else. That's why the supplier was surprised when I so quickly picked up on the unique benefits they were offering. They dedicated thirty minutes of their presentation to instructing me how to take advantage of this offer because, in their presentation planning, they weren't sure I was going to grasp the implications. Needless to say, my overreaction proved quite a relief for them. Someone else occupying my chair could have easily missed all they were saying, all the positive results that would ensue.

In each case when I decided to buy materials directly from a manufacturer or distributor, I wasn't really looking to buy direct. The benefits of buying direct just seemed to rise to the top as the best scenario during the evaluation process. I've never been an advocate for homebuilders procuring materials themselves, unless an undeniable, multifaceted benefit is attached, not just for the builder but to one or more companies in the supply chain, too.

The days of "I win, you lose" are long over. The best negotiators nowadays are the ones who can find the best alternatives for both parties at the table—especially in the production homebuilding arena where we continue working with the same subcontractors and suppliers for decades. We all want to feel like our needs are important to the other guys, too.

Many cases illustrate how I have found it advantageous to buy materials and provide them to the installer, each custom-designed to fit that local market, with its accompanying subcontractors and distributor branches. Even big, nationally negotiated agreements that include material procurement require additional local negotiations to implement. I have found it advantageous to remember that our industry remains very much a local business. Your local suppliers do not want to feel bullied by your big, national purchasing department. It's one of the biggest mistakes you could make.

Short of the few products that homebuilders regularly buy direct—appliances, light fixtures, and roof trusses—the typical relationship between manufacturers and homebuilders is limited to the administration of a rebate. The builder negotiates with manufacturers to get a rebate, a reward for using their products. Sometimes the rebate is provided in exchange for the exclusive use of their products, sometimes for the limited use. Collecting rebates is the least advantageous deal a builder has available to them. Often though, it's all we know how to do.

"To buy or not to buy"—that is the question. I don't take this question lightly, and I suspect you don't either, so what do you consider when you face it? It's wise to enlist the help of your category experts to advise you, but be careful not to ask people who actually stand to lose money (or perceive that they do) from the potential changes you are considering. You will likely find them convincing you not to do it—and for the wrong reasons.

Buying materials direct is a scary notion for homebuilders. What if we end up paying as much for materials as we did when the subcontractor bought them? What if we buy the materials and some get damaged, and then we have to replace them at an additional cost and even compensate the installer for a delay? What if the materials get stolen? Who will manage the receipt of materials at the job site? Does someone have to sign for them? What do we do when only a partial shipment is delivered? What if the wrong items are delivered? Who will do the ordering? Who should sign the invoices?

These questions and concerns (and more) are usually enough to prevent a builder from thoroughly investigating the opportunity to reduce material costs and increase subcontractor production capacity by procuring materials themselves, making them available as builder-supplied materials. And while these all pose good questions, they shouldn't prevent you from investigating this option; instead, they should help you complete a more thorough investigation.

I know people who work for multi-billion-dollar home-building companies, and the furthest extent they will take their relationship with manufacturers is to ask for a rebate. That's it. That's as far as they will ever go.

These same folks will not consider procuring materials from a distributor either for the same fears and concerns stated above. I have shared my experiences of procuring drywall from a distributor many times to some of these folks and showed them how I was doing it. They still won't try.

Even a government construction contract may contain "government-supplied materials" that the subcontractor is required to install. If the government can do it, why can't a homebuilder that has been building houses for forty years?

It's hard because of all the unknowns. Back in the 1970s when builders procured their own materials, we acquired the competency of managing those materials. As an industry, homebuilders lost that competency and have become risk-averse to the many possible things that could go wrong.

But by avoiding material procurement, you are missing out on some tremendous opportunities—not only to reduce the cost of building materials and increase the production capacity of your subcontractors, but more importantly, to significantly improve relationships with manufacturers and distributors that can contribute to your continual improvement processes. These enhanced relationships are where you will realize the most significant savings, not in a flash after some big sourcing event, but over time with suppliers who trust you.

Next, we'll calm your anxieties that may have prevented you from trying out the beauty of buying materials direct—guiding you on the path to properly analyze the opportunities awaiting you.

REBATES OR REAL MONEY?

During the Great Recession (which essentially impacted the homebuilding market from 2006 through 2011 and even beyond), I went to work for a new homebuilding company. During the interview, I told stories about cost savings achieved by utilizing supply chain management strategies. I promised to earn at least ten times my salary every year in savings for the homebuilder, which was mind-boggling to my new boss, easy-peasy for me. He asked what I would do in the first ninety days. I began with the big moneymakers: lumber, concrete, drywall. Then, after all the labor and material costs in those categories were under control, we could work together to prioritize the rest. He was very excited and hired me on the spot.

On my first day on the job, laptop sitting before me in an empty office, I began preparing for a drywall sourcing event, calling up my best strategies and eager to get started. But my boss, Steve, had other things in mind. He wanted me to work on manufacturer rebates.[16] I reminded him, "That's not where the money is. There are far better ways to reduce construction costs than rebates." He promised that, after a couple of rounds of rebate work, I could start on drywall.

For two years, I begged him to let me work on drywall, lumber, and concrete. Finally, he allowed me to move forward with what I had promised him at my interview.

Now, three years since the Great Recession started, all of our subcontracts were re-bid . . . *and re-bid again.* Our most trusted and best subcontractors were brought into the office, over and over again, with our CEO, COO, and operations VP asking them to help us with costs as best they could so we could all survive the recession together; our goal was to get everyone ready to accelerate again when the housing market came back. After multiple meetings like this, the team was convinced that our contract prices were as low as they could possibly go—and asking for more would be insulting. Steve did not expect much success in my endeavors to lower costs on drywall, concrete, and lumber.

---

[16] Manufacturers offer a volume *rebate* to those who consume their products in sizeable quantities. They consider it a marketing cost. This guarantees a significant amount of sales for the manufacturer without the usual sales and marketing efforts needed to secure such a large volume.

I worked fast, starting with the division that was in the same market as the corporate office where so many CEO and COO meetings were held. I went to each community with a tape measure and clipboard to determine exactly how much drywall was installed in each floor plan, multiplied the quantity by 9 percent for allowable waste, and came up with a total square foot quantity of drywall. With accurate quantities in hand and my database of fair labor and material prices for drywall, we were ready to call in the subcontractors and challenge them on their costs. Well, at least I was ready.

Steve was a bit shy, even a little embarrassed that we were calling these guys in, *again*. After all those high-level meetings, he felt like we were trying to squeeze blood from a stone. He told me he was going to do all the talking. The subcontractor coming in today was someone they had been working with for over twenty years and was also a good friend to many of the senior managers.

Steve started the meeting, sheepishly stating that we wanted to compare some of "Ken's" findings with the current contracts. I laid everything out in the most affable way I knew—all the quantity measurements, all the unit pricing—and simply asked the subcontractor if any of my quantities or pricing was unfair or somehow miscalculated. I was asking for his help. He went through all of them one by one, and quietly, reluctantly, concluded they were fair. That day we reduced each of the drywall subcontracts in that division by an average of $4,000 per house. And the subcontractor was still making a fair profit.

After everyone left the conference room, we put the screen projector away and headed back to our offices, still marveling at what had just taken place. Feeling lighthearted, I turned to Steve and asked, "So you still want me to work on rebates?" We both laughed and never looked back.

Steve wanted to be angry, feeling hoodwinked and somewhat betrayed. He had been led to believe there was no more margins to bargain with, only to find out a treasure chest was still left behind in each house. But the subcontractor's willingness to work with us and make all the necessary contract changes offered Steve some consolation, and he kept his cool.

During this process, we found a drywall distributor that was willing to sell us drywall while working with our subcontractor and online construction schedule to coordinate deliveries; we didn't have to get involved. Buying drywall direct ensured we were paying the right price and protected us from cost-creep if the subcontractor attempted to inch up his profit margins again.

We did not set out to procure drywall; it just happened. Our analysis left us with an opportunity to get drywall for the best price, no subcontractor markup, and have it entirely managed by the subcontractor. The only extra work for us was administrative—executing an agreement with the distributor and then paying their invoices. Piece of cake.

In retrospect, this meeting could have gone off the rails. The subcontractor could have gotten offended and combative in everything I was asserting. Thankfully, he didn't.

Instead, he was willing to let $4,000 per house disappear from his contracts . . . perhaps a big surprise to many. So why was he so cooperative and amicable?

He assumed a wide-angle perspective. He knew this was a long-term relationship, and he wanted to be part of the solution rather than part of the problem. He ended up helping us put this drywall procurement deal together, even though the benefit to him financially was non-existent in the short run. I guess he was not ready to walk out on a twenty-year relationship, and we were all hoping he wouldn't as well.

Bottom line, your best subcontractors will work with you to assuage 99 percent of the risk in procuring materials when they know your heart is in the right place. If we had taken the tough-guy approach instead of a collaborative one, we might have lost a great subcontractor. He knew we didn't want to lose him. He knew we valued his company as an extension of our own.

In the next three sections, I'll demonstrate how you can make quality decisions to implement a procurement strategy in your company without the risk you were probably presuming was linked with such an endeavor.

APPLIANCES & LIGHT FIXTURES

In an era when every aspect of house construction is subcontracted to a company that will procure the materials and provide the necessary labor, we should feel spoiled. We don't have to deal with some details: finding the right distributor, ordering, receiving, dealing with shortages, backorders, and incorrect invoices. How lucky are we? Building houses becomes tough enough without all that to deal with, too. Right?

Before you agree, before you dismiss procurement as too risky, consider what, then, would make it worth your while. What would it take to compel you to procure some of your own materials? Money, perhaps? Lots of money? Well, that's exactly what lies waiting for those who venture into this unknown area of our business. And in times of high-volume building, buying direct also becomes a method to increase the production capacity of our subcontractors or material distributors, providing you with a competitive advantage over other homebuilders.

Having experienced all the emotions of reluctance and risk-aversion, just as you might be facing, yet still compelled to procure our own materials, I think I can answer all your questions and show you how to spot the opportunities for you that are the simplest or the most lucrative (or a little of both). You are probably already doing some of the work now and don't even realize it.

One of the more common categories that many builders procure is appliances. Like everything mentioned in this book, some aspects apply to some regions, and some do not. Appliances are one that perhaps applies to more areas than most other products. At one point, though, you likely acquired the electric oven and microwave through the electrician's subcontract, and the gas cooktop[17] and dishwasher in the plumber's subcontract. At some point, if you are a builder that buys appliances direct from the manufacturer, you discovered you could save money, be supported by the installing subcontractor, and manage ordering and invoicing pretty easily.

Deciding to purchase materials and have your subcontractor install them requires a clause in your contract about builder-supplied materials. Spell this out clearly in your contract: what make/model/quantity will be supplied, how the installer will receive the materials, when ownership transfers to him, and who is responsible for any theft, damage, and wrong shipments. Nothing tricky about this; it's pretty straightforward since your subcontractor understands the gist of what you are trying to accomplish. Listen to his concerns about the method of receiving materials and the point when ownership transfers to him. If he feels like his concerns are important to you, he becomes your best resource in this whole process.

As appliances are a high theft item before they're installed, your installer will ideally install them as soon as they arrive. Sure, this requires careful coordination, but you only have to do it once. When you find the right place in the construction schedule, the installer and appliance company will manage it from there. Once up and running, the process is pretty smooth.

Establish upfront who will do the ordering, which you can accomplish in several ways: The subcontractor schedules the delivery, the builder's superintendent schedules the delivery, or the online automated scheduling system signals the delivery. I prefer the schedule to drive the delivery. That way, no one has to remember to make an order; you just have to train your supplier to use your scheduling system.

---

[17] For some readers who may not be well acquainted with this, the plumber specializes in the installation of gas cooktops due to the importance of gas connections in a house.

Builders also often buy another category of materials directly: light fixtures. And while you have a million light fixture choices, your electrician is not necessarily an expert in interior décor. This probably signifies the driving reason to engage with a distributor who knows light fixture products well, who can help with their selection, box them up (including light bulbs and cords), and deliver them as a kit right to the house.

It's funny, have you ever *deleted* something from a subcontractor's contract and found the value to be $10, but when you wanted to *add* it to their agreement, the price was $60? As you begin this process, if you are worried that your deductive change order from the electrician will not equal the amount you now pay a distributor for light fixtures, wait until the next time you bid it out competitively; it will all even out then.

For any materials you procure, put a process in place that enables a hot shot quick delivery[18] in case additional materials are needed while the installers are on the job ready to install and something goes wrong. Whether you need more materials due to loss, theft, damage, or just a shortage of parts, you don't want to hold up the installer. Payment for the Hot Shot depends on who had ownership of the materials at the time of the debacle. In my case, we over-engineered an onsite safety stock process but never even used it. If you put a good process in place, material management is simple.

It's essential to identify who is going to receive/sign for the materials when they are delivered. You can easily set this up and allow flexibility for adjustments afterward. If you set up the subcontractor as the person who receives the delivery, and he knows he will not be there on a specific day, he can ask the superintendent to sign for them, and vice versa. Whoever signs for the materials is responsible for taking a full inventory and

---

18 *Hot Shots* are an industry term to describe an urgent need for materials. Hot Shots are typically delivered in three to five hours, and include a premium charge added to the order.

immediately notifying the supplier if anything is missing. When an oversight is immediately reported, suppliers are pretty good at taking responsibility for the mistake. If you wait a day or two, you may be paying for the additional materials yourself.

Appliances and light fixtures are products you may already be procuring. If you have a process working efficiently, simply copy and paste that process for other products you deem beneficial to purchase directly—no sense reinventing the wheel.

Before moving on to the next section, write down all the materials you buy direct, either from a manufacturer or distributor. Now, answer all the questions posed earlier in this chapter (e.g., What if materials get damaged? What if they get stolen? Who will receive deliveries at the site? What do we do when a partial order is delivered? What if the wrong items are delivered? Who will do the ordering? Who will sign invoices?) and consider if your processes in place are scalable. If so, you are ready for more. If not, consider what adjustments are needed.

Next, we'll explore the process we used for procuring paint. This category is a little tricky and requires a different supply chain management strategy than necessary for most building materials.

Min/Max Paint

As I remember the story, a paint manufacturer approached us on the topic of buying paint directly from them, bypassing the painter. They offered to make a custom color for us, batching it in 5,000-gallon batches, solely for our company. Because they could batch such large quantities, we didn't have to pay extra for the custom color. The price they offered made this deal very tempting.

Yet with no track record of managing paint, we had to consider a few more factors than we did with appliances and light fixtures. For one, no two painters apply paint in precisely the same way. This means each house would use a slightly different amount of paint. How would we accommodate that variation when delivering paint to a particular house? If we provided a certain number of pails to one house and had paint left over, they could take it to the next house, but then the full delivery of paint for the next house would be too much.

Our solution? We put a Conex box[19] on the job site, filled it with two weeks' worth of paint, and gave the paint manufacturer the key to the door on one end of the box and the painters the key to the door on the other end. The supplier would push the paint into one end, and the subcontractor would pull paint forward as needed. Thus, the painter could use just the right amount of paint, whether more or less than was estimated.

Not all construction materials can be so cleanly distributed to a house as light fixtures or appliances. Some materials' usages are somewhat flexible, depending on such factors as installer technique, air temperature, humidity, and installation equipment. When we had Parker sit on the job site and watch paint being delivered and then applied to the house, he observed that some painters apply paint a little thicker and some spray it on thin. Technique, spray equipment, or both could cause differences. Either way, we needed a system that could accommodate this variation.

If this seems complex, consider that our subcontractors deal with these scenarios every day. Some crews waste more material than others, some are quite efficient, and some days require more or less paint depending on weather variations. One of the benefits of a turn-key labor and material contract is not having to worry about such things. But, if the subcontractor is absorbing paint usage variation, it makes you wonder if they are overestimating materials needed to accommodate for the anticipated difference, or when they use less material than expected, do they offer a

---

[19] Conex box is the common term used to describe a steel storage container typically used to ship products overseas. Conex boxes are also used as storage units on construction job sites.

refund to the builder? No, you likely never hear about the variance.

The Conex box includes a clipboard inside with a sign-out sheet attached. Each time a painter needs more paint, he retrieves it from the paint box and records how many pails of each type of paint he took indicating which house it was for. This process allowed us to analyze how much paint was being used in each house by each crew. Over time, we analyzed the data to discover which crews were using too much paint, not enough paint, or just the right amount. The subcontractor, never gaining this kind of information before, used it as a training opportunity for his painters. Data can produce compelling insights.

The paint manufacturer brought paint each week and pushed pallets into their end of the Conex box. The painters pulled paint from the other end as needed, enabling a constant flow of paint moving through the box. We utilized the Min/Max method[20] of managing inventory. When paint reached the established minimum quantity on hand, it triggered a need to stock up. And the manufacturer did not supply more paint than the set maximum level. Pretty simple.

This inventory method worked great. My biggest concern lay in the question of whether the painters would keep accurate input on the sign-out sheet, but they exceeded my expectations. I was impressed with their diligence.

The sign-out sheet proved necessary as we had to keep an accurate account of the paint cost for each house. A little clunky at first, the variances between two similar houses caused our division controller a bit of unease, but when we showed him the cost savings, all was well. Using this method, we saved about

---

[20] *Min/Max* is a common inventory management method that triggers an order when inventory reaches the minimum established quantity level and is limited in how much can be stocked by the maximum established quantity. The minimum level allows work to continue uninterrupted while still allowing adequate time for replenishment before running out.

$350 per house. And that included using an upgraded paint and paint color. Not too shabby.

Now on your list of construction material categories[21] that you might consider for procurement, think about including categories previously left off because the materials don't distribute evenly to each house. Chew on whether you would consider it if the benefit were big enough.

You don't have to be afraid of materials like paint. If the advantage is big enough— financially for you as well as the potential to increase your subcontractor's production capacity— I ask that you not scratch it off your list before thoroughly investigating the opportunity. You may be pleasantly surprised to discover your team already has the capacity to add this small task.

Using Min/Max inventory control methods to make paint available to painters is easy. Defining all the details upfront took some time, but it all ran smoothly after that. When the paint manufacturer first suggested this solution, something we had not done before, I think we were all taken aback, but our prior experience told us it was worth trying. Its facilitation even turned out easier than everyone thought it would be—for the manufacturer, subcontractor, and us included. Now a no-brainer, it gave a *win-win-win* all around—a most satisfying feeling.

The next section offers one more example, this time describing a homebuilder procuring a different kind of material with another twist I think you will like. Amazing . . . the difference a label can make.

---

21 *Construction material categories* typically include: concrete, lumber, fireplaces, plumbing, HVAC, electrical, insulation, windows, siding, stucco, drywall, roofing, solar panels, cabinets, paint, ceramic tile, doors, wood trim, door hardware, garage doors, stair rails, stone veneer, countertops, shower enclosures, bath mirrors, and flooring.

PRIVATE LABELING

Perhaps now you've visualized yourself procuring materials that you may not have considered otherwise. Perhaps now you've taken to heart the examples of the benefits, obstacles, and solutions for mitigating the risk of builder-supplied materials. You're now ready for another strategy that may not have been on your radar.

For years, I had a rebate program with a stucco manufacturer. I met with him often to continually explore how we could improve our business alliance beyond the rebate they provided in exchange for my pledge of exclusivity. It's not easy; the stucco subcontractors buy stucco from a distributor, who buys truckloads from the manufacturer. The manufacturer and I explored a discount, but with no way to ensure the discount would trickle down to me. The manufacturer also received no protection from a distributor who could potentially order more products at my discount rate than he was selling to me. I'm not judging the distributors as dishonest; just saying that an oversight benefiting the distributor could have been possible.

For the manufacturer to give the subcontractor the discount, hoping he would pass it down to us, also proved problematic. In a turn-key, lump-sum environment, it would be impossible to discern whether we realized the discount. Early on, we were not in a position to buy materials directly.

Then the solution dawned on us. As the manufacturer and I were brainstorming one day, he told me about the potential to privately label the ninety-pound stucco bags. This key move would ensure any discount provided by the manufacturer would trickle down to the builder as nobody else would order stucco with our company logo on it. To top it off, the discount doubled what I was getting in a rebate.

This emerged as an elegant solution, something few homebuilders have ventured to do. It stood out on our job sites, set us apart from other builders, and proved lucrative. We hung some of the empty bags in our office like a badge of honor while trying to play it down like, "Yeah, we always do this." But we didn't.

I bring up this example to help you take the limits off your thinking about supply chain strategies. You can design the methods of getting building materials to the job site in many different ways: procuring from manufacturers, procuring from distributors, taking delivery from manufacturers, taking delivery from distributors, builders ordering materials, subcontractors ordering materials—and all concluding with the builder paying the invoice. And that's key. When you pay the invoice, you have control of those costs—the primary goal of a good supply chain management program. When taking control, you open a gateway to continual improvement.

I mentioned in the last chapter that we combined stucco, stucco lath, stucco paper, and drywall on the same delivery truck and saved $1,300 per house. That combination included our private-label stucco; so, yes, we did eventually procure stucco, too. A truckload delivery would bring all these stucco products to the job site like a pre-packaged meal, all ready to cook.

Take a look at your list now, and circle the product categories where you have your best working relationships with your suppliers and subcontractors. I did not implement a single supply chain solution without their complete support. In most cases, they became our best idea-generators as we tackled obstacles. Had we scaled the terrain with a straight-arm, unilateral, tough-guy attitude, we would not have reached success. Of this, I'm sure.

The magic of transforming supply chain management in your company involves people outside your company. Building a relationship with them—centered on trust and genuine concern so we can build more houses—is what made these initiatives so fun. If we were fighting, deceiving, coercing, or forcing our suppliers and subcontractors, I would have taken no part in it. Straight out of the gate, they must know your heart is in the right place for any victories to result.

I never went looking for an opportunity to procure my own materials or private-label products with my company's logo; these results just happened through striving to find a better way. Now, the next time you sit down with a manufacturer, you will have more arrows in your quiver to find mutual benefit through the methods most lucrative for both of you.

You strive daily to build pride, develop teamwork, and create fulfilling work—all fueled by the sense that you are contributing to something worthwhile. You may have chuckled that we posted a stucco bag in our office with our logo on it, but it had real meaning to many of us. Not just because it was cool, which it was, but because of the struggle we endured to create that bag. We cultivated new relationships with suppliers and upped the game in our relationships with subcontractors, discussing aspects of the construction process we had never thought about before. These relationship-building success stories are what made it worth the late nights and weekends spent working. The end result was worth it.

In the next chapter, I'll present you with another construction supply chain strategy that is older than many of you reading this book. A home-building legend pioneered it, but then it got lost in the shuffle.

FINAL THOUGHTS: WELL DONE

A surprising twist of events left me dumbfounded. At first, the division president thanked me for the thorough job my department did in analyzing this opportunity. He was appreciative of our initiative to find creative ways to lower our construction costs. But then, with a stern voice of reproof, he launched into all the reasons why homebuilders do not buy building materials; our subcontractors do. They take all the risks—inventory management, ordering, backorders, obsolete product changes, price fluctuation, etc. He went on and on and on, as if he had spent as much time rehearsing this rejection as I had spent putting the analysis together.

Typically, before I present a new business strategy to my division president, I assemble a great deal of backup information: pricing impacts, SWOT analysis (strengths, weaknesses, opportunities, threats), potential benefits and obstacles, best- and worst-case scenarios, and lists of steps that could go awry. And this day was no different.

I brought the full package into his office and presented my case to start procuring roof tile direct from the manufacturer, utilizing roofing subcontractors only for labor and sundry materials and thus saving our company $400 per house.

And then much to my chagrin, he unleashed his disappointing response. He could have misinterpreted any attempt to argue at that point as disrespectful, so I thanked him for his time and left.

In the following days, I showed parts of my presentation to the other VPs in the office. They all loved it. The next week, I presented the entire package of information to the whole operations team, including the same division president who had reproved my proposal the prior week, and received full approval to proceed. Yes, the division president feigned to raise the issues he had laid on me just a few days before.

In his office the preceding week, right after his eloquent lecture of why homebuilders don't buy materials, I just didn't have the heart to tell him about the procurement activities the company was already immersed in—we were already procuring appliances, light fixtures, roof trusses, and engineered lumber (plywood, oriented strand board,[22] and laminated beams). I was surprised he didn't know we did this.

If you are looking for reasons why you should *not* buy building materials directly, you don't have to look far. A million reasons

---

[22] *Oriented strand board* (OSB) is a plywood-like product made from chips of wood and adhesive compressed in specific orientations. Invented in the 1960s, it replaces a lot of what builders used to use plywood for, such as sheathing in walls and flooring.

might arise to reject the idea, but there are just as many to support the idea as well. If this option has entailed a scary strategy for you in the past, consider that you are probably already doing it to some degree or another, and the processes are perhaps already set up, ready to scale to another category.

After completing my presentation, I left the operations meeting with a new directive fully backed by everyone around the table; I was to proceed with my proposal and start the process to procure roof tile. Neither the division president nor I brought up the discussion that had transpired the week before, not at that meeting nor at any future time. Later that month in a budget meeting, when we were showing the $400 per house cost reduction from our roof tile initiatives in each of the community's budgets, the division president simply said, "Well done." In my mind, I was the one saying *well done* to him. It takes good leadership to trust in your people when your gut is telling you to keep the status quo.

CHAPTER 5

Just Kitting

D o you remember the story I shared at the beginning of the previous chapter when I explained how a door hardware manufacturer proposed to put all the doorknobs and locks for a particular house into one box and ship it to the location of our choice? Well, what I didn't tell you was how they planned to accomplish it.

You see, I thought I had everything figured out. I had toured more than one hundred manufacturing plants, covering just about every product category in multiple states and several countries, so I thought I knew everything possible that could happen in a plant. Which is why it took me a minute to realize the possibility of what they were proposing.

That's when they described the plan to create a separate line in the plant—machines dedicated solely to building our products—and then pack the parts coming off that assembly line into a custom-made box. That's when it hit me: Manufacturers may not be as rigid as I once thought, and I suddenly became aware of a whole new world of possibilities. Of all my wacky supply chain ideas, none of them included an assembly line that could be changed to accommodate *me*.

I was always told that making even the slightest change to a line in a manufacturing plant involves a host of people and procedures: engineers, equipment modifications, new and re-positioned equipment, personnel training in how to use the new system, a trial-and-error period to fine-tune, and then ... finally ... maybe ... it could be a productive line. Given the complexity and allocation of resources, senior managers are tasked with proving a significant return on their investment before any changes are made. Once approval is obtained, a planning process must be carefully designed—to limit the amount of downtime or decrease the time needed to set up the new assembly line.

So here they were telling me that they could create a new line just for us, and I was honored. They had thought of my company and me in undertaking this significant commitment. I was pleasantly surprised—and amazed.

I'd always presumed that we did not merit the clout to request or even suggest that a manufacturer change their assembly line to meet our needs. The proposal up on the screen was a terrific addition to their bid, one I will never forget, one I somehow knew we would be talking about for years to come, and yes, one that sent their competitor back to the drawing board. A doozie of a proposal if I ever saw one.

Then and now, it seems that just when I think I've reached the pinnacle, when the music gets louder and I'm about to rescue the princess, another door opens . . . and I discover another level of play. As innovative and daring as I might feel about myself, as knowledgeable and experienced as I think I am, I am reminded of how many supply chain management methods to reduce costs must exist. No matter how many you discover, many more await. I love this industry.

What happened after this discovery? What transpired after I learned about a new frontier of possibilities, applying this new knowledge to achieve industry-first approaches to cost reduction? Well, that's the subject of this chapter.

It's Okay, We'll Finish It Tomorrow

Many times, I have caught myself criticizing others, not out loud but in my mind, for their self-inflicted limitations. Perhaps they worry about things that will never happen or stop themselves from doing something because they assume the worst. But this time, I was the one limiting myself by presuming manufacturers cannot make changes to an already well-oiled machine. Sometimes, I can be my own worst enemy, allowing doubts to wander around in my head, preventing me from moving forward. How many times do I have to learn this lesson?

Our industry has some real challenges. Costs continue to climb with no limiting device to stop them, snowballing downhill—from manufacturers, to distributors, to dealers, to subcontractors. Subcontractors and distributors don't have the production capacity to support high-volume building; we still are not providing houses as fast as people are being born and immigrating. Something has to change. We need to get better.

It may seem trivial that a door hardware manufacturer created a factory assembly line to support the kitting we needed. If that were the only supply chain idea we implemented, you would be right; maybe no one would notice. But when you consider this assembly-line kitting idea is just one of a hundred sound approaches to improving cost and capacity, you will find it's worth learning. Learn all of them. Learn all the approaches and strategies you can.

And when you start on that quest, I think you'll find that supply chain management is more art than science. Creative thinkers thrive at crossing the boundaries of conventional wisdom and venturing to go where others have not. And the logical thinkers make implementation possible. All hands are welcome in supply chain management.

You may remember that when I transitioned from construction operations to supply chain management, I was bent on finding a better way to get the *right materials* to the *right place* at the *right time*—every time—so that we could reduce cycle time. Kitting is one of the most essential processes to support this goal. Of all the entities in a homebuilding supply chain, manufacturers are typically the most operationally efficient. Their use of statistical process control to seek better, faster, and cheaper ways to accomplish tasks makes them our industry champions.

A subcontractor's endeavor to ensure the right materials go to the right place at the right time, every time, is frustrated by a lack of controls. *Shrinkage* alone (when employees take home products they did not pay for) describes an obstacle that manufacturers don't have to worry about as much. Consistent accuracy,[23] only achieved when a worker brings the correct quantity of materials needed to do a job on a given day, proves to be another factor challenging this goal. This discrepancy might seem insignificant, but the number of times a worker brings the rest of the materials the next day or later is tremendous. "I'll just bring them out the next time I come to this job," they say. Meanwhile, the uncompleted work is thwarting someone else

---

[23] Most subcontractors can deliver the right materials to the job site 90 percent of the time. However, because workers know that sometimes the materials won't be there when they arrive, they don't strive for on-time starts. *Consistent accuracy* in material delivery is required to warrant getting the right person, in the right place, at the right time, every time. It represents the highest level of construction-schedule discipline.

from completing their work, too, and the trickle-down effect of inefficiency continues.

Why do our subcontractors tolerate this slinky effect of inefficiency? Don't they want to do everything right the first time and not have to come back to the job site? Don't they want the subcontractor who precedes them to do his work completely before starting their work? Well, I believe this occurs because we have been doing it this way for so long, we have accepted it as the way to build houses. Only after seeing it done perfectly, without a single flaw, do the workers in the field begin to consider expecting a higher standard of performance. Those who experience the efficiency of prepacked kits of materials feel spoiled by the process and will fight to keep from backsliding to the old way.

Kitting operations, performed by manufacturers or distributors, provide a sureness to a typically uncertain process; they ease tensions for those lucky recipients who know what it's like to work without having to worry about "one more thing." Consistency is essential to convert a nonbeliever—consistency in getting the materials right, not just some or most of the time, but every . . . single . . . time. For traditional methods, this consistency proves to be a tall order, but it's a piece of cake, or pie, or whatever your fancy, for those who own the core competency of always getting it right the first time.

Ultimately—and here's the clincher—by engaging in the creation of kits, you will begin to distance yourself from inefficient practices, entice the effect of reducing construction costs, improve production capacity, and add a little peace to someone's day.

Next, we'll explore the work of an industry veteran who used kitting as one of his success secrets in creating one of the most successful home-building companies in history.

THE MULTIPLIER OF KITTING

I was talking to an electrician one day while he was wiring one of our houses, following him around as he worked. It was toward the end of the day, and he was closing down and putting away his tools. Noticing he still hadn't completed the bathroom wiring, I asked if he were going to stay late and finish it up. "Naw," he said, "I forgot to bring out one more bathroom exhaust fan, and I ran out of ground clips. I'll bring them out tomorrow on my way back from tomorrow's job and finish it all up."

We reminded him that he was supposed to be done today, and he quipped that the plumber wasn't done either, so insulation couldn't begin until both of them were finished. He felt he had more time. Maybe the plumber was thinking the same thing? I wonder if that's one of the ways we lose days in our schedules.

To the electrician, this was no big deal. It happens all the time. That's how he always performs work. To the homebuilder, the same. For a supply chain manager bent on making things better, my imagination began to wander.

Parker, my colleague, once asked if we could put together kits of materials so installer workflow wouldn't be interrupted due to forgotten items. By this time I had learned not to say "no" to Parker. We soon began meeting with electrical distributors and found out they already assemble kits for some of their commercial construction customers, especially those working on government contracts. This new solution was going to be much easier than I expected.

Kitting refers to assembling a group of materials together before sending them to the job site, creating a package with all the electrical parts needed to rough wire a house, for example. Or putting all the HVAC parts together on a pallet or two. These include parts that come from multiple manufacturers, and while typically procured separately, they can come from the same distributor or sometimes various distributors. The separate parts are often sold to subcontractors in case quantities, forcing the subcontractor to keep an inventory so they can break down cases and allow the tradesmen to pick out the materials they need for the day, hoping they don't forget anything. As for kitting operations, though, the distributor puts all the parts for one single home on a pallet. The installer doesn't have to think about it.

An interesting note about this: Michigan State University has one of the best supply chain management programs in the country. The name of the college that administers this program is the Eli Broad College of Business. Eli Broad is one of the founders of the Kaufman and Broad Home Corporation, now called KB Home. Kaufman and Broad made their entry into the homebuilding market by building homes at budget-friendly prices, allowing buyers to have mortgage payments that were lower than the rent of an apartment. What was the primary supply chain strategy that Kaufman and Broad employed to achieve a construction process enabling a low sales price? Simple answer: kitting. They continually experimented with different material kits but kept kitting as a strategy for quite some time.

By the end of our investigation, we were ready to roll out a new procedure for delivering electrical materials to the site, complete with everything needed—which saved money and increased the installers' production capacity. The support from suppliers, who had already been doing this for years, as well as dedication from our friendly electricians, made this one of our smoothest implementations.

In his book, "The Art of Being Unreasonable" Eli Broad said, "People who accept the status quo and conventional wisdom don't really make a difference in the world." Applying this philosophy to his own homebuilding company, he said, "The conventional wisdom in Detroit was that no one would buy a house without a basement. We challenged that, built homes without a basement but with a carport, and it was an instant success." The Kaufman and Broad Corporation sold six hundred homes in their first two years in business.

Today, some might say that conventional wisdom says to leave material management alone. If it ain't broke, don't fix it. Whether you consider our homebuilding operations "broke" or not, arguing that no room for improvement exists proves difficult. Today, costs and production capacity are not meeting the needs of all the people who need a new home.

As you may have noticed on your job sites, a somewhat lackadaisical attitude prevails about finishing the last 10 percent of a construction worker's tasks. That's why the best construction managers, those particularly good at getting the final 10 percent done in a timely manner, are highly valued. Our observations revealed that not having *all* the right materials at the *right place* and at the *right time* is one of the leading causes of an installer finishing late. Simply improve material management, and you will improve an installer's *job complete* performance.

When we toured warehouses of several electrical distributors, witnessing their robust kitting operations, we learned how a *Pick 'n Pack operation* could be better than we could have imagined. These guys were good. Before our eyes, they demonstrated how fast and easily they could complete a kit for rough electrical or finish electrical installations.[24] Because the process required so few of their resources, the price to create the kit remained minimal.

Most of the employees, all former electricians, guided us through the process of installation, justifying the materials in the kit and their placement, whether on the top or at the bottom of the pile. They kept using the phrase "hit the ground running" to describe the enabling effect the kits gave the electricians. It proved impressive.

Measuring the effect of increased production capacity is complicated. For an installer who wants to finish his work a day

---

[24] *Rough electrical* refers to the wiring behind the walls, before drywall covers it up. *Finish electrical* parts include the switches, receptacles, light fixtures, and circuit breakers installed after painting is complete.

earlier, one less trip to the warehouse can make all the difference. Instances of when the warehouse is out of the way or something was forgotten and requires a trip back to the shop again all chip away at his chance to do things right the first time. I'm an advocate for having the right people on the proverbial bus. I believe our industry is better off when installers are installing, and supply chain managers are managing supply chains.

Parker, a fresh set of eyes, was seeing things that most of us construction veterans could not. His questions, unassuming yet provocative, opened the gate to an entire platform largely overlooked for decades, offering the real help we had been searching for: cost reduction and increased production capacity.

Entrusting suppliers to deliver ready-made kits magnifies the production capacity of installers. Certainly, you will do it for the money as large cost savings ensue, but you will *keep* doing it for the efficiency it brings to your construction process.

In the next three sections, I'll show you several different approaches to kitting—each demonstrating various benefits, challenges, and obstacles to implementation—to round out your understanding of kitting for homebuilding.

ROUGH & FINISH ELECTRICAL

For the builder who has been managing contracts, not materials, for his entire career, the responsibility of assembling a kit with a miscellany of parts and pieces prescribed by craftsmen can seem overwhelming. Especially when we barely know the materials' makeup, where they originated, and how they are handled. We need to know how a particular material is inventoried and placed in position, the right position, at just the right time, and how an order is fulfilled by one or more suppliers—all requirements that add incremental danger for creating backorders and ordering mistakes. As a builder who has been subcontracting everything, the mere mention of your intent to procure kitted materials and supply them to your subcontractors will incite anxiety from just about everyone, internally and externally, colleagues and subcontractors, even the friends you meet up with for lunch.

I am happy to tell you—in every instance, pilot program after pilot program—an overabundance of caution was considered in the design (and over-design) of the kitting and delivery of pieces and parts, not to mention the safety stock created for every community in case of failure at any level. In the end, safety stock was never used, and everything we worried so much about never happened.

Time after time, more and more people involved in the pilot became believers in the process as a new best practice. Especially those with an in-depth understanding of the way it used to work: the craftsmen who installed them. What better testimonial could you have?

In this section, we will take a more detailed look into what it takes to put rough electrical and finish electrical kits together, and the unexpected buying opportunity we stumbled upon.

The decision to provide materials to our electrician produced an unexpected effect. What was once an ordinary builder-subcontractor relationship now included a flip-flop in roles: Yes, when builder-supplier materials are involved, the electrician can become the customer to the builder.

We all know that before you can attempt to satisfy the needs of a customer, you must discover what those needs are, and the best method is easy: Just ask him. I found that electricians, arguably the most educated of construction workers, are usually pleasant in all dealings and interactions. Electricians communicate better than most of the folks on a construction site, and they listen well when you talk about a new supply chain management initiative that can improve business performance.

Show him how your new initiative will benefit him—getting the *right materials* to the *right place*, at the *right time*, every time—relieving him of procurement, inventory, and last-mile deliveries to the house. Engage your electricians in the process by having them generate a list of all the materials they need. Then delete some of the small parts that carry over from one house to another that accrue a minimal cost, like wire nuts, ground clips, and zip ties. The quantities from one floor plan to another will change, but the variety of products stays about the same. Once you have the list and quantities, you are ready to meet with distributors to find out how much this will all cost. It's time to go shopping.

The electrician's list of materials cannot come from anyone but the electrician awarded the contract. Electrical, like HVAC, plumbing, and framing, are design–build contracts—meaning the builders do not design this portion of the house, a subcontractor does. A builder supplies the floor plan and some guideline specifications, and the electrician combines them with building code standards to develop an electrical plan. Each electrician will create a design slightly different from another; that's why he is the only person qualified to provide a material take-off list for a particular house.

Collaboration with your electrician will ensure you have the right bill of materials (BOM), and that's important, but more importantly, it will engage him in the process, making him part of the solution and enlisting his willingness to make it work. This single step, by far, proves the most critical. A disgruntled electrician made to feel like others are dictating demands will surely make the process fail. This illustrates another area where I have learned that straight-arm, tough-guy tactics do not work. Collaboration is the key to success here.

When creating electrical kits for the first time, you'll find it good practice to engage multiple electricians separately to learn what you need to know to make the process successful. Various electricians will think of different things, giving you a more rounded understanding of their actual needs. Before you "go live", collaborate with your electricians one more time. This extra step proved beneficial for me because I was constantly adjusting the plan and needed them to see it in the final state.

An electrician came up with the process of how to manage copper wire. Similar to painters, no two electricians wire a house precisely the same. Differences emerge from one house to the next, even with the same electrician wiring the same floor plan. For example, in one house, he may have to route wire around an HVAC duct to get to a room; in another, the HVAC duct was routed differently, necessitating a different electrical route. An electrician suggested we assign a base amount of wire of each type in the rough electrical kit. Then, if he has wire leftover, he will take it to the next house until the quantity of leftover wire is substantial enough to warrant an adjustment to the BOM. If he runs short, a Hot Shot of wire will be sent to the job, and the wire quantity in the BOM will be adjusted likewise. Significant discrepancies, in wire or any other product, are corrected to all BOMs during this process. Similar to the scenario with paint, this cost variance aggravated our controller until I told him we saved an average of $542 per house with this supply chain method. Needless to say, he was okay with the minor variances.

Before you can ask distributors for a bid, you must qualify them. In several aspects of kitting for residential construction, they need to prove proficient before prices can decide the contract recipient. This task is pretty easy; once they understand what you are trying to achieve, they will disqualify themselves if they don't think they can do it.

First and foremost, you need a distributor who can assemble kits. All of them will tell you they can, so arrive at their shop early in the morning and observe them putting kits together for other customers. You'll be able to ascertain, especially when comparing three or more, if kit assembly rises to a core competency for them or not. Ask to speak to a few of their customers who use their kitting services.

It's also essential for the distributor to remain willing to sell materials directly to you, the builder. I recall a first meeting that pretty much tanked. This distributor was already supplying materials for many of the electricians with whom we had subcontracted. At least one of these electricians, who did not like the idea of using builder-supplied materials, told the distributor that if they sold products direct to us, he would never buy from them again. Blackballed.

That distributor shooed us out of their shop so fast. The other three distributors, who at the time had very few residential customers, were quite happy to welcome new business. Two of them had kitting operations that impressed us beyond our loftiest expectations. By limiting the number of steps to create kits, they were extremely efficient, touting a 98 percent or higher fill rate. Most impressive.

Once you get beyond a distributor's willingness to work with you and gain an understanding of their kitting abilities, you are ready to send them a Request for Quote (RFQ) for each of the kits for each of your communities. Remember to include Hot Shot pricing, just in case you need additional materials to cover loss, theft, or inaccurate BOM. *Establishing Hot Shot pricing up front saves you high dollar charges when they are required.*

After we had awarded contracts to two distributors, we spent time with them designing the workflow. That's when the unexpected happened. One of the GMs asked me if I wanted to pay the market price for copper wire or make ninety-day commitments, enabling me to make more significant buys when the price was lowest. "You can do that?" I asked.

He said, "Sure, your electricians do it all the time." Instantly, I wondered if we ever received the benefit of those great buys. I don't think we did; I think the electrician charged us market price for copper wire and pocketed any advantages he made on his speculative buys. Over the next few years, I made a lot of money for my company by taking advantage of the low curves in copper pricing, consistently buying an average of 4 percent below market prices.

One-quarter of your electrical cost is for copper wire. A 3,500 SF house has approximately 8,750 feet of it. If you build 2,000 homes each year, you are buying over seventeen million feet of copper wire. At the time of this writing, a 4 percent savings on wire equates to about $700,000 per year (at $1.00/LF for 12/3 type wire). Being successful at buying copper futures requires doing your homework on the copper commodities market and is not for the faint of heart. You may, from time to time, end up paying more than the market price within your ninety-day buys, but I found it well worth the effort.

Yes, we navigated a myriad of obstacles in finding the best supply chain strategies for electrical—subcontractors that renounced the builder-supplied materials process, a distributor that kicked us out of their warehouse, a dire need to create BOMs with no electrical plans, as well as plans for when things went wrong including Hot Shots and safety stock. Yet the single biggest hurdle centered on creating *organizational change*. More specifically, I had to get emotional buy-ins from my coworkers (and then subcontractors and distributors) with the biggest naysayers originating within my own company. Tradition creates a powerful magnet.

While you were reading this, I hope some ideas popped into your mind. List your ideas about kitting, about your relationship with electricians, and about how to create organizational change. Write them all down. Think about which electricians and communities would comprise your best candidates for piloting a program like this. Now, think about your internal resources: Who would be best to put on this team?

With that brainstorming now underway, you're already off to a great start; you're on your way to actualizing an excellent supply chain method to reduce construction costs and increase production capacity.

HVAC

One day I was having a one-on-one meeting with a subcontractor in my office. The purpose of our meeting was to discuss whether he was willing to use builder-supplied materials. As we were discussing this proposal for about the seventh time, I was already talking to some other companies, relatively confident this subcontractor was still far from agreeing to the terms.

He seemed noticeably nervous, though I wasn't sure why. No, I wasn't going to terminate his contracts if he didn't comply. But I admit, if we found a good subcontractor demonstrating success with a job or two, a danger for this subcontractor would solidify; we would not give him any *new* contracts. Of course, we had spoken none of this aloud, but from his response, I suspect a swarm of negative thoughts were abuzz in his head.

One of the steps in converting a turn-key contract to include builder-supplied materials entails deducting those materials from his contract. To do so, you have to mutually agree on the value of those products. That's what this meeting was about.

Fearful that he was about to give away his company's most treasured secrets, he slowly slid a piece of paper toward me. For each of the materials we had discussed, it listed unit pricing removed from his contract. I had been working on this particular project for about a month, so I already knew the fair market value of those products. Yet I kept that cat in the bag.

I looked down at the paper, quickly scanned the prices, looked up, and thanked him for his willingness to be a team player. I told him I would review his pricing and include this data in assessing the feasibility of utilizing builder-supplied materials for his construction category. One thing, however, caught my eye: He could have found better pricing at the local big box lumber store on some of those items, and the others weren't that great either. I could easily beat all his pricing with the deals I was working on with manufacturers and distributors.

Why didn't he know that he could have gotten better pricing at the subcontractor's desk of Home Depot for some of those items? It's possible that he was not truthful in exposing his real pricing, just to see how I would react. But I don't think so. I think he was sincere. Somehow, his distributor(s) convinced him that he was getting great pricing, and he believed it. This experience, and many more like it, changed my belief that subcontractors that specialize in one construction category are all champions in all aspects of that category. This new perspective compelled me to ask more questions and not assume subcontractors know everything they needed to know. Their specialty lies in the installation of those products, not necessarily the source of screaming deals.

With the experience of kitting rough electrical and finish electrical kits under our belt, we were eager to clone the process for other products. Our next target surrounded the HVAC category. With fewer parts than electrical, it didn't seem too challenging. Was I in for a surprise?

Our objective with HVAC, like every other category we explored for optimization possibilities, focused on satisfying a make-or-buy decision. The make-or-buy decision, as used in home-building operations, entails whether to choose builder-supplied materials (make) or to include them in a turn-key subcontract agreement (buy). It resembles a manufacturer's choice to manufacture one of their needed components or to procure it from an outside source.

We began by acquiring a parts list from the HVAC sub-contractor. Similar to electrical, this is a design–build contract in which the HVAC design is not provided by the builder but by the subcontractor. Once we had the parts list, we visited every local distributor that would accept our invitation to collaborate. Some were willing to meet with us, and some were not. That's okay.

We explored the kitting idea with each of the distributors willing to listen to our unconventional ideas. Some of them thought our ideas were brilliant; others, not so much. That's okay, too. We ended up with two distributors ready and willing to provide the kits we proposed. Each of them practiced and practiced until they perfected the kitting process. They found efficiencies in their operation, which lowered their costs to assemble, and we had a final product—accurate kits at a price lower than what the subcontractors were charging us, all ready to purchase. Yet . . . we chose not to do so.

We already enjoyed a substantial rebate from the equipment manufacturer, so the cost we would have saved on the ducts, registers, and line sets[25] was not worth the effort for us to manage the materials. I think we would have saved about $70 per house, but some liability in the delivery and receiving process seemed a bit risky. We decided the risk was not worth the savings potential.

Our subcontractors loved the idea, though, and since the kitting operation had already been developed, they started buying kits from these two distributors. As we were the homebuilder that facilitated the development of this process, they split the savings with us, lowering their contract prices and improving their production capacity. Such a boon for everyone! As this scenario illustrates so well, when a builder can provide the leadership to influence a better deal with their upstream suppliers and subcontractors, it's still considered a win. And consistent with my findings with other implementations, when you help your subcontractors reduce their cost of doing business, they will be happy to share some of their good fortune with you.

Our HVAC installers all had more than twenty years of experience. Then, if this was such a great idea, why hadn't they done this a long time ago? I asked them this question, and they admitted they were entranced by tradition, never thinking to question the current process. Now, after experiencing this, they question everything.

Kitting proves that an old concept works as well today as any other supply chain management strategy—just as long as you find the right balance of cost and benefit and include that balance for your installers, distributors, and manufacturers. In every case

---

[25] An HVAC *line set* is the high-pressure copper tubing that runs from your outdoor condenser to the coil attached to the air handling system inside the house.

I've witnessed thus far, an increase in the subcontractor's production capacity ensued. In times of tight labor constraints, this increase alone can offer a homebuilder enough justification to pursue facilitating kitting operations.

Similar to each of the runners in a relay race, every step of the construction process can add or subtract from optimal efficiency. Whether you are motivated by lowering costs, increasing production capacity, or both, make the effort to continually find an extra second here and there to finish the race with a new personal record.

PLUMBING

Do you remember my story of the seven little words that wrecked our industry? A plumber stood in my office, pleading with me to help him reduce his overhead costs, and I interrupted him by saying, "I don't care; just get it done." George was complaining that if we added another brand of faucets to our specifications, he would have to lease more storage space to hold the additional inventory of faucets and extra parts.

Not until years later, after I discovered the possibilities of kitting, did it occur to me: I could have solved his cost issues, which became my cost issues, with kits assembled by distributors. Distributor-assembled kits can relieve the plumber from having to procure case or pallet quantities of materials and store them in his warehouse. Or, at the very least, it can significantly reduce his inventory needs.

Plumbing installation in residential construction includes three main phases. First, before the concrete foundation is poured, drain lines are positioned in just the right place with just the proper slope to allow for drainage. Next, after the walls and roof are framed, those drain lines are extended up through the walls, and piping is run to sink, tub, and washer locations. Finally, after the ceramic tile is set in the showers, after the walls are painted and the cabinets installed, it's time to install the sinks, toilets, and faucets. The first two phases can become a little tricky to kit. Drain lines are often prefabricated in a plumber's shop, and not many parts are included in the water lines operation. Kits can be assembled, but not easily.

The most significant opportunity here entails the finish plumbing stage. Providing all the finish products accurately and neatly on a pallet could save a plumber much time and opportunities for mistakes. Imagine all the toilets and sinks on one pallet, and the faucets, tub/shower trim, and medicine cabinets all neatly stacked on another. This scene becomes eye-candy to a plumber who has to remember to put all the right parts in his truck every day, and when he forgets something, has to go back to the shop to get them. How many trips back to the shop would it take for you to get frustrated? Keep in mind, plumbers only get paid when installing, not when driving around.

The sky's the limit to possible combinations of plumbing phase products that could be kitted, but here's another one to think about: While the plumber is installing sinks, toilets, and faucets, the electrician is installing switches, outlets, and light fixtures. What if one distributor could kit them all together, neatly, so each subcontractor can easily access them? I no longer believe that a distributor cannot kit products he doesn't know anything about due to my experience with door hardware and light fixtures, drywall and floor tile. So then, why not include HVAC finish products, too? Registers, grilles, and thermostats are being installed at the same time the electrician and plumber are installing their finish products. Ohhh, the possibilities.

Subcontractors have taken on the responsibility to buy materials in bulk and have the installers load up their trucks on the way out to the job each day. Every one of them believes he has better pricing than his competitors, aided by his bulk buys and shop inventories. In my experience in supply chain management, about 15 percent of subcontractors are really good at managing materials and negotiating excellent pricing. The rest do an okay job. Why is the gap between my perspective and theirs so different?

I have learned to look at material procurement and management in a different light. I view the whole house of materials all at once; subcontractors are only focused on one category, preventing them from ever coming to the same conclusions as I have. As far as pricing goes, I found that distributors are more willing to give you a better price when they feel their needs are important to the builder. The subcontractor who rarely gets the best price often buys from whoever is cheapest, continually changes his orders after placement, and doesn't pay his bills on time. These are the subcontractors that could benefit most from builder-supplied materials, reserving their energy for what they are good at: building houses.

List the product categories that you think might work in your area. Be adventurous. Anything too off-the-wall will work its way out during the vetting process. Besides, you'll learn valuable lessons while vetting just about any kitting possibilities— experiences that often lead to lower future construction costs. Consider the category experts in your company, including the strength of relationships with subcontractors, distributors, and manufacturers, to help you decide what to work on first. If you feel you don't know enough distributors, utilize your connections with manufacturers; they can point you to some of the best ones.

Generally speaking, plumbing, electrical, and HVAC include some of the most challenging materials to optimize. Builders can feel helpless with categories designed by someone else, making supply chain management even more daunting than before. Kitting is one area where you can make a difference, though, with decreased costs and increased production capacity in these elusive categories.

In the next chapter, I'll paint a picture of how communication from homebuilders to subcontractors, distributors, and manufacturers, works and doesn't work, formulating the single most consequential opportunity for improvement to our industry.

FINAL THOUGHTS: JUST A BOX OF LOCKS?

Early one morning, I watched a carpenter go about his business on the job site, a rewarding time of reflection for me. The carpenter was most likely oblivious to the monumental task that had gone into creating the box of locks that he picked up so routinely. But not me. I was riveted to the scene.

After heading inside with his box, he then walked around the house, pulling out the doorknobs and locksets and setting them on the ground next to each door where he was about to install them. It all happened perfectly, like a symphonic performance on a Friday night.

Just to see it for myself, I arrived at the job site at 5:30 am. I was waiting for the door hardware and light fixtures to be dropped off so I could see what the process looked like in action. At 6:15, a truck drove up, dropped several boxes on the driveway, got a signature, and was gone as fast as he came. The carpenter installing the locks was already there.

I could never have imagined that a box of locks could be so gratifying. We saved money and increased the production capacity of the carpenter; everything we wanted. We made changes to our systems to allow a new door hardware SKU for each floor plan we built. The new SKU included the assembly of doorknobs and locksets required for each house. That's unusual, and it took some process and programming changes. While we were doing that, the manufacturer created a whole new assembly line just for us. The subcontractor adjusted his methods, too. I didn't count them, but I'm sure thousands of hours of work went into that first box of locks.

Reflecting on the accomplishment of kitting a box of locks, wondering why I felt such a tremendous feeling of satisfaction, I realized it wasn't the money or the increased capacity that so pleased me. It was the new closeness we developed with our *new, expanded team* in creating this industry-first method. Many people were involved, from IT to construction superintendents, from manufacturing plant managers to assembly line workers. It took tremendous effort to pull this off, some of it during working hours and, for some of us, a great portion through after-hours and late-night toil. Most of us were pushing against the wind the entire time, no coasting, to create these new processes. We had bonded together in a unique cross-company way.

It didn't take long for the carpenter to install all the locks. It's incredible how fast installers can work. I looked around for something else to do in that community while there, but I found nothing more. So I sauntered to my car, turned back to look at the house I just left, and thought about how great it felt to be part of something special. I love this industry.

CHAPTER 6

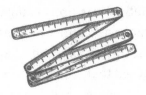

Demand Signals

itting in a conference room full of industry giants, I could feel the electricity rippling through the air. In yet another round of supplier meetings at the home office, the next supplier was one of our industry's most sophisticated manufacturers, known for loaning out their employees to help train other companies on Six Sigma,[26] a process improvement strategy that seemed brilliant. Each person they brought to this meeting had VP in their title or it began with C: COO, CFO, CPO, Operations VP, Sales VP. I was a regional VP of Supply Chain Management, the most junior title in the room.

---

[26] *Six Sigma* is a data driven methodology to continually reduce defects in a manufacturing process or eliminate waste in a business process.

The supplier was there to bid on gaining our exclusive use of their products for the next three years. But this assemblage of corporate honchos marked an unusual entourage for such an occasion. Typically, suppliers are represented by a sales VP and one or two others that have developed a good relationship with someone on our side of the table. This many high-caliber officers could only mean one thing: They wanted this contract badly.

The presentation was proceeding as anticipated until someone from our ranks asked them a question about manufacturing operations—one that broke the eloquent flow of their heady offering and caused their countenances to go pale and foreheads to furrow. *The response to such a simple question will likely be general in nature,* I thought, *and we'll pass over it like a comment about the weather or their breakfast toast.*

We asked them, "How do you know what to make and when to make it?"

These folks are world champions at using Six Sigma: statistical process control, control charts, and process mapping to continually improve operations. I know this because they trained me years earlier as a Six-Sigma green belt. And they were the best trainers around. Their response to this question, after much starting and stopping, stuttering, and side-to-side glances was basically, "We guess." We *guess*?

Or in the long version, they said something like, "There aren't enough demand signals from our customers (input) to ensure we will make the right product at the right time (output), so we're sometimes either forced to hold inventory that won't sell or lose business due to backorders. Therefore, we use Six Sigma methods to help us guess incorrectly less often."

If a sophisticated manufacturer like this can get it wrong, not knowing what to make and when to make it, what does that say for other manufacturers in our industry? Before this meeting, I had always assumed that manufacturers knew what to make. I admit to seeing inventory when doing plant tours, but I believed it was the desired inventory needed to ensure a steady flow of products to their distributors.

We discovered that manufacturers do not like inventory— of any kind—on hand. They consider inventory part of a distributor's responsibilities, not theirs. We also found that backorders typically occur because the manufacturer didn't know that a particular model or color would create more demand than anticipated, not because they ran out of raw materials or couldn't make products fast enough.

Corroborating their assertion that homebuilders impart few demand signals, they said they clock about 10 to 20 percent more efficiency with their big box wholesale and retail customers. These customers usually give them a two-month lead time on orders, detailing the make, model, color, and everything needed to optimize manufacturing operations. In essence, homebuilders could be paying far less for products by simply sending better signals that enable manufacturers to make the *right thing* at the *right time.*

We just learned that changing the way we communicate orders can affect a price reduction of 10 to 20 percent. Not just we, but all homebuilders would have to comply with this new standard to sufficiently influence a reduction in the cost of doing business. I thought to myself, *we can do this. The obstacle is not that big, compared to all the things we do to reduce the cost of building houses; all we have to do here is communicate better.*

Years before, when I learned my lesson about not listening to subcontractors who were trying to tell me I was the cause of my own high prices, why didn't I ask the obvious question? *Are we doing something that is costing manufacturers money, too?* The answer would forever change my outlook on how homebuilders should communicate demand signals to the supply chain.

We realized that distributors and manufacturers are hungry for demand signals required for optimizing operations, and this realization forms the core of this chapter.

24 TO 48 HOURS IS NOT ENOUGH

In the early 2000s, the company I worked for was building 40,000 homes per year. We used the same kitchen faucet on most of them: the Moen 7560c. With access to the online construction schedules, we could tell you exactly how many 7560c faucets we needed in the next ninety days. But do you know what we told Moen? Nothing! Our only communication with Moen was requesting rebates for home sales that occurred in the last quarter. We had always assumed that our subcontractors were communicating demand to distributors, who were aggregating demand for all their customers and sending the information to Moen.

Come to find out, subcontractors usually order products just twenty-four to forty-eight hours before they need them, even though they know what's required almost ninety days prior, completely squandering any chance for the manufacturer or distributor to optimize operations.

So when a high-performing supplier walked into our conference room and admitted they *guessed* what to make and when to make it, all the conjecture suddenly made sense—and we became resolved to fix it. Relying on subcontractors to communicate demand up the supply chain was not working, and thus we learned a valuable lesson: If we're to become better communicators, it's up to the homebuilder to make it happen.

This experience caused us to evaluate the quantity and quality of communication up the supply chain, leading us to conclude that, in actuality, a multitude of communication points were never getting past the subcontractor. Knowing how much money each link in the supply chain could save through better communications, we were motivated to find a way to improve— and influence other builders to do the same. The manufacturers are the ones who told us that *no matter our achievement in better communications, if the whole industry doesn't change, lower prices can't be realized.* In fact, *the scale must be large enough to affect the majority of their business,* they said.

Building houses isn't easy. Keeping costs down while doing it? Even harder. With all the cost-saving opportunities available to you, how do you know where to start? Start by helping your supply chain take cost out of their day-to-day operations. Make contributions to enable your manufacturers to make the *right thing* at the *right time.* Help your distributors reduce their stock inventory without causing more backorders. I know it seems counterintuitive, but you start by caring more about others than yourself. Then your prices will go down and continue downward as you keep working together as a team to reduce each other's costs.

Really? You may be asking yourself if all this holds water. Doesn't making a concerted effort to take cost out of your suppliers' operations, helping to improve their profit margins first, seem like a fool's errand for a homebuilder? Our industry has about 48,000 residential construction companies, over 400,000 specialty subcontractors, and about 45,000 building material wholesalers, making us one of the nation's most fragmented industries. Creating a communication protocol that enables some level of consistency in how messages are sent and received is no small task—but desperately needed if we are to lower the price of building materials.

Most builders don't consider the needs of suppliers, those responsible for the materials needed to build their houses. Instead, we expect our subcontractors to cover that component. If you're like us, this information will lead you to conclude that relying on the competitive bid process—between builders and subcontractors, and between subcontractors and distributors— may not produce the results so crucial to winning the fight on rising construction costs. We need a better way.

Why do homebuilders continue to rely on subcontractors to perform the critical task of effectively communicating up the supply chain? Most likely, a scenario similar to when I threw those seven little words ("I don't care; just get it done.") at my plumber may be occurring up the supply chain. And if so, then like my plumber, they long ago stopped complaining about the pain points that drive prices up.

Consider the perspective of the subcontractor who purchases products for one specific construction category for which he has a contract. The builder has the view of the whole house. So who is better suited to drive communication throughout the entire supply chain? I believe we have mistakenly put this task on the subcontractor when, in fact, it's *our* responsibility to lead this effort.

In the end, communicating SKU and Date Needed data is not the most challenging hurdle a builder could navigate. All we need to do is learn to communicate better, which includes active listening to the suppliers we haven't yet met.

JUST-IN-CASE INVENTORY

Dan, a new wholesale distributor to our company, was starting to open up to me. For the past two months we had been meeting every week, a valuable time of relationship-building that I had initiated. I wanted to know what kinds of things builders were doing that cost him money, and he was slowly warming to my earnest intentions.

At first, he simply gave polite, general answers, not actionable, not sincere. Yet each time we met, he provided another puzzle piece regarding the pain points of running a wholesale distribution company. Each week he became more convinced of my sincerity to learn. After a couple of months, he was telling me things about his company that his employees didn't even know.

One day, as Dan and I were walking the aisles of his warehouse, observing the racks filled with products, all neatly organized, labeled, and accessible, we approached a pile of products in the very back. As we got closer, Dan steered us in a different direction, pointing to things that kept my back to the heap that had piqued my curiosity. But before we lost sight of the mysterious pile, I stopped and asked, "What's that?"

"Those are the D's," he offered.

"The *what?*"

Dan's warehouse was organized like most others. In a staging area close to the loading doors, products were arranged by customer order, ready to be loaded onto trucks. To keep warehouse foot traffic to a minimum, Dan placed the A items, those purchased the most, on the storage racks closest to the staging area. The B items were next in proximity to the staging area, and those labeled C were products ordered least frequently and placed farthest from the loading doors. Thus, as employees rolled carts around the warehouse filling orders, this system enabled them to fill more orders per hour than if the products were placed randomly.

Now seeing he could no longer avoid the inevitable disclosure, Dan reluctantly told me the D items were those products he couldn't sell. Nobody wanted them. Yet he had ordered them because he thought the builders were going to use them in their houses. This pile of products represented incorrect *guesses* of what he should stock. The D products were not only eating up the money to pay for them, but taking up valuable space in the warehouse. And, on top of that, they required human resources to manage them.

Inventory costs money. The stock unable to be sold comprised one of Dan's more costly pain points. Now he had to offer deep discounts to move them, or worse, throw them away.

Like the suppliers who dragged their feet, so hesitant to admit they had to guess which products to make and when to make them, distributors find themselves in the same boat. Of course, they do their best to make a *best guess*, using historical sales data and anecdotal information from salespeople, but still . . . it's just a guess. When you have to guess, you're going to err some of the time. And that costs all of us money.

In their reluctance to admit their less-than-perfect methods, I could see their unhappiness drenching their words. Both manufacturers and distributors are often starving for more information about what builders are going to order in the next thirty, sixty, ninety days. Builders have the information at hand; we just don't share it.

What these suppliers were not telling us, however, was exactly how much this communication malaise was costing them. When asked, their facial expressions shifted from reluctance to embarrassment. Thankfully, their expressions changed again when we proposed putting them on our electronic construction scheduling system, giving them access to each product needed on every calendar day for the next ninety days. Actually, they started glowing.

Just as every builder would love to know exactly which floor plan, amenities, exterior elevations, and driveway length their customers will pay the most for, our suppliers ache for insight into which products we will be ordering. The difference here is that we have the information the suppliers want. We've got the ball in hand, but instead of passing it to them to enable teamwork, we're playing keep-away.

Good drivers are not made by simply pointing a car in a straight line and stepping on the gas or brake as needed. A skillful driver is someone who is good at predicting what other drivers are going to do. Therefore, if we want others to be good drivers too, we must drive predictably, using our brake lights, turn signals, and flashers when needed. Reliable supply chain management emerges similarly—it requires a certain degree of predictability to reach its highest efficiency and smoothest flow.

The residential construction industry comprises a predictable sector of construction, with the predictable repetition of homebuilding often proving tantamount to satisfying a person's need and craving for "delectable meals" and "balanced nutrition." When we learn to share vital information that could quell the supply chain's "hunger," we will reap a tremendous benefit in the form of lower prices and fewer backorders.

As I mentioned, we discovered that a great deal of money lay at our fingertips, ready to be made through more effective communication. For our manufacturers, coming up with a solid figure of the value of *advance demand signals* proved easy as they also had big box stores as their customers, who consistently order products far in advance of required delivery schedules. For other manufacturers and distributors, however, doing so proved more difficult to imagine. The distributors with whom I had worked most closely estimated they could save 8 to 20 percent with advance data. This estimate included reducing the size of their warehouses; they would need less inventory to supply the same number of products. Then again, if their prices dropped that much, maybe their sales would increase and warrant stocking more inventory.

Your own situation may require some back-office system changes in order to provide the information vital to increase the efficiency of distributors and manufacturers. It will also require you to convert from lump-sum to unit-price contracting, but you need to do so for most other supply chain objectives anyway. The power lies in your hands. Simply by communicating SKU and Date Needed information to manufacturers and distributors, you can decrease the price of building materials as much as 20 percent.

Next, we will explore the communication needed to achieve this tremendous efficiency—from the perspectives of a sub-contractor, a distributor, and a manufacturer—helping you see what it will take to implement this vital strategy in your company.

SUBCONTRACTORS

It sounds simple: Just improve communication between you and your suppliers, and you will save lots of money. But most of us know that the dynamics of relationships can prove challenging.

Communicating well is not as easy as it sounds, with unspoken expectations one of the leading causes for "divorce."

However, in supply chain management, you've got an advantage: Certain signals effectively trigger specific actions. Once you know the actions that your suppliers are waiting to take, it's easy to understand the signals they are waiting to receive. Then you can focus on improving your ability to send the *right signals* at the *right time*.

Homebuilders have been communicating directly with subcontractors for a long time, with the purchasing department talking to them regularly about contracts and change orders. The construction department talks to them sometimes multiple times daily, ensuring they are correctly interpreting the signals we're sending them. The aim of all this communication results in the desired action of building our houses on time and on budget.

Much of this communication is electronic, only supplemented with discussions to tackle exceptions as they occur. We connect them to our online construction schedules, we connect them to our automatic purchase order system, we connect them to our repository for drawings, specifications, color charts, plat plans, and everything else needed to perform their tasks.

Subcontractors have everything they need to pass on the SKU and Date Needed data desired by distributors and manufacturers. But in most all cases, they don't pass it on; it stops with them. Instead, subcontractors filter the information and only pass on data that support their immediate needs—nothing more, nothing less.

I mentioned earlier that subcontractors don't order materials, nor do they let anyone know they are going to do so, until twenty-four to forty-eight hours before they need them. This practice isn't done to impede the supply chain's ability to optimize but rather to enable the highest cash flow potential for their company. Issuing a purchase order to a distributor triggers a time clock to begin counting down the days an invoice is due. Subcontractors often wait until the last minute to order materials, hoping to install them and get paid by the homebuilder before the invoice is due, preserving cash flow as the end game. Otherwise, the subcontractor has to pay the invoice out of his operating cash, and many of them don't have much of that.

Many subcontractors define success as having enough cash flow to support ongoing business, and at the end of the year when they do their taxes, they discover whether they made money or not. They compete to get as many contracts as possible, do their best to perform adequately, and make no waves to attract attention. No news is often good news.

Running the hamster wheel just as fast, the homebuilder considers adherence to the construction schedule vitally important. They avoid delays at all costs to deliver the house on time to the homebuyer. So when a subcontractor experiences a backorder of material, they often do their best not to let the builder find out. They will try to get started on their work, but stall somewhat while they wait for the backorder to arrive. One reason for not telling the builder? They know the first question a builder will ask is, "When was it ordered?" and then they'll get no sympathy when it's discovered they ordered it yesterday. Only when a distributor or manufacturer openly admits they are the reason for the backorder will a subcontractor bring it to the builder's attention. That's one reason why homebuilders remain unaware of how often backorders occur.

These days, computers perform the task of sending repetitive information. Homebuilders have been using electronic schedules and purchase order issuance since the early 2000s. Distributors and manufacturers also depend on technology for managing both the movement of upstream materials and downstream tracking of goods sold, as well as the support of their day-to-day operations. Some of our subcontractors use their sister-in-law's email address to do business and manage most of their crew scheduling on whiteboards.

I have visited hundreds of subcontractors' offices to learn what's important to them. I remember one time I was scooting around a desk and came dangerously close to wiping my back against a whiteboard completely full of data used to manage their company: Builder Name, Community, Crew, Date, etc. All at once, every person in the room gasped. Alarmed, I froze, and then moved slowly away from the whiteboard. I offered to whip up a spreadsheet to manage the process, but they preferred whiteboards.

It's essential to recognize that technology supports operations for builders, distributors, and manufacturers, but not so much for subcontractors. A whiteboard and a cell phone are all a subcontractor needs to run a business. Once a homebuilder recognizes this fact, it's not hard for him to create processes to push SKU and Date Needed data past the subcontractor to where it's badly needed. But the homebuilder, not the subcontractor, must take the initiative. If you wait for subcontractors to get good at using technology to communicate with the supply chain, you will be waiting a very long time.

Yet here's the rub: With many categories, and depending on your estimating process, subcontractors might be your best source of SKU data. They are often the only keeper of this crucial piece of information, further driving the need for homebuilders to convert to unit-price contracts.

Subcontractors, when ordering so close to the time they need materials, become susceptible to backorders. And because subcontractors know that delays will make the builder mad, they will try to get materials from another distributor if their regular source has a backorder. They will also purchase from an alternate source if they think they can save some money. Frequently changing distributors at the last minute can also frustrate the distributor who is trying to predict which SKUs and quantity of SKUs he needs in his warehouse. I'm not saying subcontractors should always single-source and stay loyal to one distributor; I just want to point out that it can complicate a builder's desire to reduce pricing with supply chain efficiencies. The subcontractor can find it advantageous to decide which distributor to utilize at least thirty days ahead of time.

To illustrate a key point, one of my teenage sons totally wrecked my car while hurrying to get to a photoshoot. Attempting to arrive at the early morning shoot on time, he had to travel a long way on a road notorious for bumper-to-bumper morning traffic. On this road, traffic often speeds up, then suddenly comes to a stop, speeds up again, then suddenly stops, like a slinky. If you don't keep a safe following distance, you risk crashing into the car ahead of you. If you do keep a safe following distance, other cars will swoop in, filling the gap. Rear-end accidents happen on this freeway every single day. My son did not get hurt in the accident, but I lost a great car.

You could also use this slinky effect to describe a subcontractor's procurement habits. Always ordering at the last minute, they sometimes order a lot and sometimes order nothing, making it challenging for a distributor to predict the demand and still have the products subcontractors need when they need them.

As illustrated, vital supply chain communication has to be initiated by the homebuilder. Don't blame your subcontractors; you hired them to build your houses, and that's precisely their skillset. Expecting them to comprehend the whole house, the entire supply chain, and change behaviors to find efficiencies may prove unrealistic. The homebuilder remains the logical choice to author effective supply chain communication.

DISTRIBUTOR SIGNALS

Like most business owners, Jimmy loves his customers. Since the day he opened his store, he has been resolved to provide the best customer service his contractors have ever seen. Jimmy sells a variety of building materials to specialty subcontractors at wholesale prices and carries about $7 million worth of inventory.

Once a subcontractor enters his store, Jimmy does his best to meet all their needs. He listens carefully to what they say, seeking to discover products they are buying from other stores, and then he brings those new lines into his business to give his customers as much of a one-stop shopping experience as he can. Jimmy makes money when he has at least seven inventory turns per year. Carrying products that don't sell is one of his major obstacles to making money.

I was chatting with Jimmy at the far end of his service counter while we watched his employees take care of customers. One guy, obviously unhappy that Jimmy was out of stock of something he needed, left without buying anything. Jimmy knew where he was going: to his competitor down the street. This worried him; he knew that once a customer starts buying materials somewhere else, he could lose that customer forever.

Unfortunately, his customers order products twenty-four to forty-eight hours before they need them—barely enough time to process the order and stage the material for pick up or deliver it to the requested location—leaving no time for planning or optimizing inventory. Jimmy does inventory optimization planning based on guesses of what he thinks will sell in the coming months. When I asked Jimmy how he decides which SKUs and their quantities to stock in his warehouse, he said he uses historical sales data combined with anecdotal information from his sales staff, and then makes his best guess. He told me he guesses correctly "sometimes."

I asked Jimmy to imagine what it would be like if most of his orders were submitted sixty days ahead of time. "Are you kidding?" he asked, and then added something like this: "If I had just thirty days, I could optimize my inventory and only carry what I knew would sell, significantly increasing my inventory turns and issuing my customers fewer backorders. It would be better for me and way better for my customers because I could lower my pricing."

I asked Jimmy how much he could reduce his prices, and he had to think about it for a couple of weeks. When he got back to me, he estimated that if he had orders sixty days ahead of time, he could reduce pricing by 5 to 15 percent.

When homebuilders start construction on a house, it typically takes thirty days to build the foundation and another thirty to frame it. It's not hard to imagine giving every distributor sixty-days' lead time on orders. The concrete and framing crews plan for the start of a new house at least thirty days before construction begins, giving them ample time to allow inventory optimization to occur for their distributors and manufacturers, too.

Isn't it amazing that we could save 5 to 15 percent on pricing by merely changing the way we communicate with suppliers? It seems like a small investment for such a substantial return, but how do you accomplish it? The homebuilder who builds houses with turn-key subcontractors doesn't even know who the distributors are. How can you possibly manage a timelier ordering process?

Several possibilities await. You could inform all your sub-contractors how important it is to communicate orders at least thirty days in advance and urge them to comply. But here's the caveat: They may feel hindered from losing the chance to switch suppliers at the last minute to save a few dollars, and thus they may end up charging you extra for the money they thought they might lose from this restriction. Dictating a business process to thirty-five subcontractors, expecting they will all do it well, is challenging. And, if successful, how would you know if the price reduction were passed on to you and not kept quiet by the benefiting subcontractor?

One of my first ideas was to issue a zero-dollar purchase order to each distributor and manufacturer, providing a view of the materials in our unit-price subcontract agreement and their quantities, without causing chaos for accounting. The purchase order issued to your subcontractor would contain all the SKUs, their quantities, and associated pricing. A zero-dollar purchase order could be issued to distributors and manufacturers with the identical SKUs and quantities but with no pricing, preserving the confidentiality of pricing between you and your subcontractor. I would have to collaborate with my subcontractor to negotiate pricing up front with a particular distributor so we wouldn't have to switch at the last minute. Often, the subcontractor and I had to promise fast-pay to get them to agree. That's all these suppliers would need; the SKU and Date Needed data would enable them to significantly optimize their operations.

One obstacle we quickly stumbled upon involved the list of materials. Amounts ordered by the subcontractor were not precisely the same as shown on the zero-dollar purchase order we issued. In our early days of converting to unit pricing, we phased in the level of detail in the zero-dollar purchase orders. At first, we only had sheets of drywall on unit pricing. Later, we broke it down further and added joint compound, joint tape, and corner bead. Then later, we added screws, nails, and caulking. These iterations happened over two years. During that time, our zero-dollar purchase orders required some manual inter-pretation on behalf of the distributor. They had to use calculations to determine the missing materials proportionate to the amount of drywall ordered. This scenario is better than having orders come in twenty-four to forty-eight hours before you need them, but not as good as having all the materials on a document that doesn't require manual interpretation.

After experiencing a myriad of obstacles and a lot of trial and error, we concluded that technology would be required to make this possible. Computers don't sleep, have bad days, or make mistakes, as long as the programming is correct. We needed our back-office system to manage unit pricing and allow us to send zero-dollar purchase orders. Both of these steps took significant effort from our IT department, but once completed, it ran smoothly.

A smart distributor will take it a step further and write a software interface to electronically absorb your zero-dollar purchase orders and use the data to include in his inventory optimization strategy. The goal for him lies in reducing his just-in-case inventory—products that he purchases *just in case* someone were to order them. That's how you take cost, not margins, out of the supply chain, which translates to sustainable lower construction costs.

Zero-dollar purchase orders may not prove a viable solution for you. However, maybe you can generate a report that provides a list of products and quantities the distributor will need. A solution exists to fit every builder, subcontractor, and distributor in each market; you just have to find it. Homebuilding is a localized business, and often these solutions need solving at the local level. In any case, those who want the reward will make an effort to find the right solutions to enable this powerful cost-reducing strategy to succeed.

When I asked distributors, "What is it we do that costs you money?" I received an earful, all revolving around communication to enable inventory reduction and elimination of "D" inventory. Distributors in our industry love their customers, but they would like them more if they communicated on time and paid their bills on time. Homebuilders can undoubtedly help with better communication.

Have you ever driven behind a two-footed driver: one foot on the gas and the other resting on the brake? They often rest their foot ever so slightly on the brake pedal, unaware the pressure is just enough to light up the brake lights. With the brake lights on and the car maintaining speed or, even worse, accelerating, the surrounding drivers are left confused. They don't know if the two-footed fiend is starting or stopping, slowing or accelerating. So we learn to drive using only our right foot so we don't send the wrong signals to surrounding drivers; they need those signals to predict our movements accurately.

Building material distributors thrive on demand signals to help them know what products to stock. When subcontractors order at the last minute, or change their order two or three times within the first forty-eight hours, or cancel their order and change distributors at the last minute, they send all the wrong signals—and in the end prevent Jimmy from effectively optimizing his inventory. When homebuilders help them nix the confusion and send demand signals distributors can understand and act upon, optimization soon follows. With lower pricing right behind.

MANUFACTURER SIGNALS

Manufacturers don't have to guess *what* products to make and *when* to make those destined for big box stores. The purchasing agents for large stores know what products their customers will buy and thus will send orders to the manufacturer in plenty of time, allowing for optimization of raw material procurement, the manufacturing process, and shipping operations.

When it comes to products bound for residential construction sites, however, the best a manufacturer can do is combine historical sales data with anecdotal information from sales reps, and then make their best guess. They know the guess will be skewed, but guessing is better than no decision at all. They make their decisions on raw material and component parts in advance of the actual manufacturing. Assembly line operations depend on useful data to enable an optimized, no-waste process. In the long run, if the data isn't helpful, they will expend materials and labor to make products that don't sell.

Manufacturers, like distributors, can benefit significantly from increased communication of SKU and Date Needed data. Thanks to the rebate program, a lot of high-volume builders already have contacts at many manufacturing companies. Now it's time to change the typical conversation between homebuilders and manufacturers, transforming talks of rebates to the exchange of SKU data.

Some raw materials and component parts are sourced overseas, requiring a manufacturer to order them far in advance of knowing what homebuilders will be ordering. Yet this involves a gamble. They may select the wrong parts and thus tie up capital resources, take up space in the factory, and in some cases, hold onto them until they're obsolete—just to throw them away. Some raw materials have a short shelf-life, adding further risk to all the waste.

Manufacturers often use an assembly line for multiple products. They run products on the line until they meet the quantity goal, then make changes to the line and run another product. These line changes are similar to a race car pit crew changing tires and adding fuel as quickly as possible. Downtime on an assembly line is like watching a price meter on a gas pump—you're just counting the dollars ticking up . . . and up . . . and up, with no stopping until assembly for the next product starts. Before any changes are made on the line, decisions are considered carefully. Yet without good data, they are just best guesses.

Each time a manufacturer orders the wrong raw materials or makes the wrong decision when optimizing the people and equipment on an assembly line, money is wasted. Each of these inefficiencies adds to the overhead costs of a manufacturer, who includes these costs when determining sales prices. The less effective their guesses, the more they have to charge for products, passing the cost of inefficiency through the distributor and subcontractor and straight to the homebuilder.

Homebuilders hold the key to helping manufacturers make a marked improvement to their operations. SKU and Date Needed data will help them know *what* products to make, including colors, *how many* to make, and *when* to make them. With this data, they may decide to make a large quantity of a particular product, either because they got a good deal on raw materials or because they want to run straight without changing the line, gaining the maximum amount of operational efficiency. Or they may decide to do just-in-time manufacturing for a fuller optimization. Whatever option is selected, they'll be making decisions with good data—no more guessing.

Communicating SKU and Date Needed data with manufacturers is similar to what you might do with distributors. It could be done with a zero-dollar purchase order or perhaps a custom report. Either way, the report should be electronic so the manufacturer can absorb the data into their Material Requirements Planning (MRP) software. They will likely build an interface to enable computer-to-computer communication, no humans involved, except to analyze the input data and make operational decisions.

The manufacturers with whom I've done all this are perhaps still jumping for joy, dancing on the table, happy about what we accomplished. I had no idea how incredibly important this data was to them or the significant impact it would make on their business. They used it to improve nearly every aspect of their company: raw material procurement, manufacturing operations, manufacturing capacity, inventory, shipping—*and no more backorders.*

All these efficiencies contribute to lower prices. The manufacturers with whom I've worked or discussed this opportunity agree that there is the potential of a 10 to 20 percent reduction in price when they can operate this efficiently. I'm reading between the lines here, but I think this acknowledgment was their way of telling me the big box pricing is 10 to 20 percent below mine. I was amazed that timely demand signals could have such a profound effect.

If we take 15 percent off the price from the manufacturer to the distributor, and then take 15 percent off the price from the distributor to the trade contractor, we have just reduced the cost of building materials by about 28 percent. This gives a high average. Savings will be less for some products (e.g., lumber and drywall) and more for others. Either way, it's a lot of money.

Sometime later, in another conference room, you should have seen the look on their faces when we described the ability to broadcast SKU and Date Needed data. Other builders have talked about it, and some have tried it, but it never came to fruition.

When we described our successful pilot with a hardware manufacturer, their entire countenance changed. For the first time, they believed that builders and manufacturers could collaborate and continually improve processes to lower each other's costs. When the company president threw his hands out to both sides with his VPs sitting beside him in the conference room, and he said, "This is a different deal! This is different! This is what we've been looking for," we knew we were on to something big. And so did they.

Every cool thing I achieved with distributors and manufacturers was successful because of the collaborative work we accomplished with subcontractors. They are the folks that build our houses, and no matter how smart your supply chain management methods seem, you still need your subcontractors to buy in and become part of the solution. In the next chapter, we'll explore some ways to motivate subcontractors to play an integral part of all your supply chain solutions.

Final Thoughts: A New Team with the Same People

My first attempt to provide SKU and Date Needed demand signals to a manufacturer encompassed the most work of any other effort. Our back-office system was JD Edwards,[27] and we needed some custom programming to get it to function adequately to support SKU data. We also needed some modifications to our third-party software that married our construction schedule activities with the SKU data, and yes, we paid for those modifications. The manufacturer wrote an interface to accept data from our third-party software into their MRP; they paid for

---

[27] *JD Edwards* is a back-office accounting software owned by Oracle. It is one of the more common platforms used by large production homebuilding companies. While its common usage is for accounting, it was designed to be a whole enterprise solution, including for supply chain management.

that. After a great deal of custom programming, we were ready to go live.

I had just negotiated an amazing deal with a door hardware manufacturer. Not the same one I spoke of earlier, a different one. This deal included a box of locks too, patterned after the initial hardware deal I had executed years before. This time, though, technology was involved.

Finally, we did it. After a long journey of custom programming, basic function testing, software code reviews, and user interface testing, we had a finished product, ready to enable computer-to-computer communication between a homebuilder and supplier. Bypassing the whiteboard schedules of our subcontractors, but not excluding them from the process, we accomplished this as a team effort. We created a new definition of *team*. We had never previously considered distributors and manufacturers as part of the construction operations team. We do now. And we couldn't have done so without the unselfish determination of everyone involved.

This accomplishment signified a first for our industry, as far as any of us were aware. That wasn't the only reason we were gratified by what we had done. Being first may have been a motivator to get us started, but we were fueled by a team that worked long hours every day to benefit the person next to us. This bonded us together in a way I cannot put into words. This new definition of team made me jump out of bed each morning, eager to get to work.

The work we accomplished enabled a single manufacturer to receive demand signals directly from a homebuilder in one product category. Yet it comprised just the tip of the iceberg; the new system has no limit on the number of suppliers we could connect to. We reduced our construction costs and set ourselves up to revolutionize our supply chain, and along the way, developed some of the best friendships I've ever had.

The head of the IT department, the manufacturer representative, and I were finished for the day. This was our last day to work together; no more meetings. The next time we would all sit in the same room together would be . . . probably never. We high-fived, hugged, shook hands, and tipped our hats several times before we actually got out the door. I didn't tell any of them, but I didn't want it to end. I didn't want the project that brought us all together—solving problems we only recently learned existed—to ever come to a close. Yet we each went out the front door and turned to go our separate ways, climbed into our cars, and left.

I look forward to every time our paths cross. What a great time to be part of such a wonderful industry.

CHAPTER 7

Subcontractor Relations

There I stood, peering out from the other side of the counter where "Employees Only" get to go. I was welcomed into the framing subcontractor's office, not the foyer or conference room, but the place where decisions are made and non-essential people are kept out.

Mark had been awarded several contracts from my company, so he brought out graphs, notices from suppliers, and lumber lists for those communities. We were going to make strategic lumber buys together. I had to pinch myself to make sure this was all really happening.

Throughout my twenty-something year career thus far, I'd never seen subcontractors invite general contractors into their office to discuss internal operations. I had mostly been in commercial construction at that point and had worked for a production homebuilder only a few years; recently, I had accepted the role of purchasing manager. So I wondered what this welcome into the subcontractor's "inner chambers" really meant.

In my experience to this point, I saw most subcontractors doing their best to get as much, or take as much, from a general contractor as possible, including omitting some information so they could capitalize on change orders later. At the same time, general contractors did their best to push subcontractors' prices down as low as possible, having subcontractors bid against each other by using other coercive methods until the general contractor felt satisfied he had nothing left to squeeze. In this win-lose environment, each player sitting on opposite sides of the table tried to do their best to win, causing the other to lose. Commercial construction, I realized, can be a cold business. But was residential just as contentious? From my welcome by Mark and his crew, I was somewhat amazed.

Now in the production homebuilding industry, I was certainly open to the fact that I had a lot to learn. I knew what it was like to work for a general contractor whose employees do all the construction work, and I knew what it was like in the dog-eat-dog commercial construction business, but what was happening here? I couldn't believe what was happening. Was this normal?

To make the best decisions about strategic lumber buying, we also had to consider the overhead costs of Mark's framing company. The time equipment is left on a job without construction activity is costly; He showed me his prices and what it costs him when his equipment is idle. The supervision of a job site, even when framing work was inactive, consists of multiple people, and he showed me those costs, too. The danger of delivering lumber to a site and not beginning framing operations right away can lead to theft, and he showed me how much theft was costing him each month.

We met at his office for hours, making strategic lumber-buying decisions on about nine job sites, including the current and near-future phases for each of those communities. As we were finishing up long after most folks had gone home, I realized what had just happened. A subcontractor trusted me enough to open his books, show me pain points that drove strategic decisions, and considered me part of his team. Until this moment, I didn't know that was possible.

This chapter is devoted to sharing how to strengthen the relationships between subcontractors and homebuilders, leading to higher quality work, lower prices, increased production capacity, and most of all, a tremendous sense of camaraderie.

No More Mr. Tough Guy

After more than twenty years in construction, I was admittedly frustrated with the level of detachment a general contractor has with the people doing the building for him. Sometimes, it seemed we would even wish for their demise if it included a potential benefit to our job site. Often, we joked that *the subcontractor awarded the contract is the one that makes the most mistakes or omissions on his bid*. He had no chance of making money, but we didn't care; he was legally obligated to do the work—and for such a low price at that. Yes, a rough culture permeates some aspects of commercial construction, though some situations are better than others.

You can see why this meeting on the other side of the service counter at a subcontractor's office seemed so foreign to me. It was the kind of thing I was hoping for when I decided to change my career to production homebuilding: a warmer business. But I admit, this profound and rare welcome was far better than I'd expected. In fact, this experience was the beginning of a new me. From then on, I wanted all subcontractors and homebuilders to work this closely together.

It just makes sense. If you were a homebuilder that did construction with your employees and all procurement was done by your internal team, wouldn't you use the same criteria that Mark and I did that day to make all your purchasing decisions? Why then, would we abandon that scenario and force our subcontractors into making less than ideal choices, accepting the reality that they pass on any extra costs to us? We frequently rely on the competitive bid process to achieve the lowest price, but if all subcontractors are equally inefficient, we still pay for it.

A better way exists to keep pricing down and quality up— increasing the production capacity of our construction force. Certainly, I was lucky that I accepted my first homebuilding job with a company that fostered a culture of collaboration with its subcontractors. The environment proved fantastic for employees as well as subcontractors, material suppliers, and designers alike.

I was exposed to how the process should look right from the start. As a superintendent, I was particularly surprised by the level of high-quality craftsmanship. The tradespeople took pride in their work and strived each day to do their best. It made my job easy, allowing me to take on other responsibilities. I loved it.

My experience stood out as distinctive and unique. Most folks in my position use the carrot-and-stick approach to motivate subcontractors. Mostly, it's the stick: "Do this or else . . ." Even in residential construction, back-charging subcontractors for damages incurred on the job, whether they are responsible for the damages or not, has commonly been considered one of those sticks.

When subcontractors feel they are treated unfairly, they tend to adjust their actions to match our expectations, and both parties perpetuate a culture of adversarial reciprocity. Of all the tough-guy negotiations and sticks used to motivate, I have never seen results that came close to the effectiveness of a collaborative, all-one-team approach as my employer, a renowned homebuilding company, had achieved. And that's why I was invited behind the counter.

Once you've experienced the difference between adversarial and synergistic relations, it's hard to go back to the tough-guy approach. In addition to excellent business results, the gratification of working together as a team proves rewarding in itself.

News travels fast; negative news travels faster and adheres to everything. It doesn't take long to gain a reputation as a tough guy, a builder who prioritizes their needs before others with no concern for whether subcontractors make money or not. A few of my prior bosses in commercial construction were convinced that if subcontractors were not mad at me, I was letting them get away with too much. I've done some pretty dumb things to appease my boss's expectations. Never again.

Nobody comes to work with the intention of doing a lousy job. For this reason, we should look to blame the process, not the person, and fix the process that causes an undesired result. That's the perspective behind this key mindset and supply chain solution. We always need to keep in mind that subcontractors are people too, who are part of our team to achieve success and gratified by their contribution to building houses, people's dreams.

LISTENING LOWERS COSTS

Here's another conference room story that I think offers some enlightenment. This time, the operations teams sat in a conference room with sales data and construction schedules in hand, with the purpose of adjusting those construction schedules. We were carefully considering the sales pace for each community and the opportunity to raise prices on future phases. We studied the staffing capacity of sales, construction, and customer service personnel and made final decisions on changes to our construction starts.

As described in the opening pages of this chapter, I had recently discovered how it felt to meet behind the counter of a subcontractor who considered me part of his team. And as illustrated there, we practiced the habit of consistently claiming we valued the collaborative relationships with our subcontractors. However, here we were, about to make decisions that would affect the operations of 137 subcontractors—without including them in any part of these decisions. Yet when I suggested we should seek their input, I was pummeled by everyone at the table, arguments flying about how much complexity it would add to our process and the difficulties that would ensue.

Everyone—except for the division president. "You're right. We need to include them," he said.

Soliciting their input turned out to be less work than was thought. We sent a letter of proposed construction schedule changes to every subcontractor and asked if they had any reasons why we shouldn't proceed because of cost implications or other challenges. Most responded by saying all looked fine, and a few proposed some adjustments to some of the changes. All, however, were honored by our reaching out to them before pulling the trigger.

What the operations team deemed an insurmountable task and far too complicated to tackle turned out to be a relatively simple step that advanced our mission to cultivate an atmosphere of teamwork and inclusivity. Subcontractors, like any of your employees, want to be heard. When you consistently demonstrate you are listening, they keep talking. When they suspect you don't want to listen to what they have to say, they stop talking—and add the higher cost of your decisions to their next bid.

In contrast, sending a letter to all your subcontractors, informing them you're taking 10 percent off each invoice and contract, does not lower costs; it reduces profit margins. Continually rebidding to find a lower price increases subcontractor overhead costs. Homebuilders will succeed better by shifting the focus to reducing costs, not margins.

Listening lowers costs. Sounds trite perhaps, but I don't care. It's one of the most valuable lessons I've learned in my career. Subcontractors are a homebuilder's frontline operations team. They know better than anyone else how to improve operations that will produce lower pricing. If they aren't talking to you now, start asking questions . . . and keep asking; eventually, they *will* open up to you. Often, they are itching to tell you things.

The key to convert listening skills into lower costs? Act on what they tell you. Show that you value their opinions by taking action on the concerns they bring up. As they see you taking action, they'll gain confidence that you will use the information to make improvements, not against them in some way, encouraging them to open up more. It takes time—more for some than others—to get comfortable telling a homebuilder that something isn't right. It takes courage—both on their part and yours—as they share their pain points and you respond by *asking sincere questions* and then *adjusting your operations* to meet their needs.

The seven little words that have plagued the homebuilding industry—I don't care, just get it done—have taken their highest toll on our subcontractors. When you begin asking, "What is it we do that costs you money?" homebuilders can discover effective ways of reducing the cost to build a house, which frequently require the least amount of effort to implement. In other words, low investment, high yield ideas.

When subcontractors believe their needs are important to you, they will give you a competitive advantage with their best crews and best pricing. Working together to solve issues they care about will result in lower costs, higher quality workmanship, and an increased production capacity. They know how to do it; they just need someone who will listen.

In the next three sections, we will consider some of the most important issues brought up by subcontractors, as well as the solutions we found most effective in advancing mutual benefit.

JOB READINESS

The job of a drywall subcontractor is straightforward: Install drywall on the walls and ceilings, tape the joints, then sand and texture. No other subcontractors are working inside the house during these thirteen days; they get the whole house to themselves. When bidding on a new job, the drywaller trusts they will have the entire thirteen days, including 100 percent of the first day. This allows him to estimate the least amount of labor necessary to complete the task, helping him achieve the low bid needed to get the job. Once awarded the contract, he relies on having a job site that promotes maximum efficiency, because if one thing goes wrong, it quickly eats into his profit margins.

One of the unique facets of production homebuilding is predictability. This trait stands as important in configuring the lowest bid to get awarded a subcontract. Ability to get started on the first day of your work's scheduled duration proves so important that a phrase has been created to describe it: Job Readiness. This term is used to hold preceding subcontractors accountable to complete all their work before the next subcontractor begins his.

The term Job Readiness has been used to describe the completeness of a subcontractor's work. It implies the next crew on site will not be hindered by incomplete work, a messy site, or obstacles left behind that affect their ability to hit the ground running. Most subcontractors have a common goal: finish their work as fast as humanly possible and get to the next job site. This efficiency is what a construction worker perceives will maximize the amount of money he can make in a workday.

Sometimes subcontractors must choose between making more money or getting home earlier, but they want the choice to be theirs, not one mandated by the circumstances of incomplete work or a mess left behind. One of the worst scenarios a worker sees affronting him involves the need to come back to finish something on another day. Frustration arises amidst the waste of having to go back and complete something simply because another subcontractor didn't complete his work before you began yours. And, unless you're an hourly worker, you don't get paid to go back and complete unfinished work. You only get paid to install a fireplace once. Going back to complete your work ends up being on your own time.

Want another tip that may seem obvious—but is often overlooked? Everyone needs a checklist. Just as an airline pilot uses a checklist before takeoff, a subcontractor should use one, too. A house has many parts, so relying on everyone at the job site to remember each item needing completion before going home is problematic—at best. I have seen examples of Job Readiness checklists from many homebuilders. As long as you have a continual improvement process in place, you can start with any checklist and continue to fine-tune it with your superintendents and key subcontractors. Here's the objective: Cover all the items that are important to the succeeding subcontractor. For a time, we made the signed checklist part of a subcontractor's final pay. They had to get it signed by the superintendent, signifying all items were completed on time before we gave final payment. I still think that's a good policy.

Subcontractors all over the country consider Job Readiness as one of their top concerns. To increase its success rate, the report card and payment checklist systems both prove effective tools for homebuilders to use. Each requires a single communication between the homebuilder and one subcontractor, but even that isn't always needed. Sometimes, communication on a job site is so good, everyone knows the tasks needing completion and are motivated to accomplish them.

This focus on Job Readiness reminds me of a story from my past. As a sprinter on my high school track team, I learned that the slowest part of a relay race is passing the baton. To increase your running speed throughout your leg of the race, you can work hard and make small, incremental improvements by tenths of a second. Yet with just a little practice, you can save multiple seconds by reducing the time it takes to pass a baton and get to full speed sooner. This collaborative work—with the runner both before and after you—proves essential to a successful relay. The gratification of faster race times pales in comparison to your elation when all four of you pass the baton flawlessly. Feeling connected as a team while achieving a high-level performance proves so fulfilling, it makes all the hard work and practice worth it. The term "relay *team,*" not "relay *racers,*" describes the relationship you have with your subcontractors—and the relationship they have with one another. Any efforts you make to ensure that team remains in tune reaps finish-line celebrations.

Yet subcontractors with adjacent tasks in a construction schedule typically don't collaborate closely with each other. Not because they don't want to. More likely, they don't feel the need. In other words, they don't see one another as part of the same team. They presume that if everyone just goes out there and does their job, there's no need for chitchat. No need to heighten communication. Yet it's a lost opportunity for optimizing crews, for reducing the amount of time a house sits empty, and for consolidating material deliveries.

In other words, subcontractors generally operate independently of each other. They comprise separate companies with their own business strategies and employee expectations. These expectations may or may not conflict with the other subcontractors on the job site. Nor would they even know . . . unless they spent time seeking to understand each other. Unless a problem arises, they likely won't even learn each other's names. These are good folks, just focused on different objectives.

A homebuilder can create an environment of teamwork that makes it easier and more desirable for workers on the job site to work together. I once worked for a homebuilding company that very nearly went bankrupt. At the eleventh hour, a private equity firm swooped in and provided a boatload of cash. With the cash also came a new interim CEO. His name was Ken—I liked him from the start. After about three weeks on the job, Ken called an all-hands meeting. He stated his three goals as the company's interim CEO.

First, he wanted to make us one of the most profitable homebuilders in the industry. Considering we almost went bankrupt, that statement brought some astonished glances, yet in three weeks, things had already started to turn around. It seemed feasible.

Second, he claimed we would have the highest customer satisfaction scores in the industry. We had already made some significant strides, so that was believable, too.

Lastly, he said we would have the highest employee satisfaction, measured by *Fortune Magazine*'s "100 Best Companies to Work For." Yet in addressing this goal, he stated, "I can't help you with this one."

You could hear the audience gasp.

He said, "When each of you comes to work each day with the intention of making this a better place to work for someone else, this will be the best place to work." He was right.

Ken's philosophy on how to make a company the best place to work extends beyond the workplace. When each member of a neighborhood intends each day to make it a great place to live for someone else, it becomes the most desirable place to live. When the students and faculty of a school intend each day to make it a great place for someone else, it becomes the best school in the district. When the members of a religious congregation intend each day to make it a better place for someone else, it becomes the best church you have ever attended.

I have witnessed homebuilding communities where everyone is committed to making it a great place to work for someone else. Sun City Shadow Hills exemplified one such community—the first time in my production homebuilding experience I witnessed the electrician grab a ladder for the carpenter. Or the plumber grab an extension cord for the HVAC guy.

Shadow Hills was a high-velocity housing community; we started four homes and finished four homes per day. The construction cycle time? Just sixty-seven days. The velocity was so fast that the workers rarely left the job site. If I'm not mistaken, I think the drywall crew worked there every day for about five years, never moving to another job site. And they developed a stronger relationship with our superintendent than they did with their company managers. Certainly, this illustrates a unique situation, but the lesson learned proves invaluable: Construction crews can achieve more work with fewer resources when they work well together.

Ken exuded modesty in his statement that only we could make it a great company, that he alone could have little impact. You see, strong leadership is needed to cultivate an environment where high performing teamwork can flourish—leadership to communicate a vision in a way that motivates people into action.

The facilitation of such collaboration among subcontractors requires strong leadership from the homebuilder. The subcontractors cannot create a collaborative culture on their own, or at least not to the same extent as when the homebuilder leads the way with equal commitment. It's easy to underestimate the importance of passing the baton well, but once realized, the satisfaction derived becomes a craving. We discovered that the benefit of this synergy on a job site equates to lower prices and shorter cycle times. Every time!

PODDING COMMUNITIES

Each community of homes is typically scheduled as a stand-alone project with no consideration for other projects nearby. Imagine if the guy that installed a fireplace could drive to one of your nearby communities five miles away and install another one. This would limit his driving time and increase his installations per day.

He would also make more money and potentially contribute to shortening the construction cycle time.

Yet even when builders have good intentions to create connections like this, they often have trouble doing so consistently. While each community tends to be isolated, I discovered the great potential in capturing efficiencies when considering all your region's communities as one big project or several medium-sized clusters.

I don't think anyone would dispute that putting three jobs out to bid simultaneously, in one lump, could reap better pricing than bidding them one community at a time. The challenge comes in doing it. Once the clock starts ticking on the interest payments for the land, it's a race to the finish line. As soon as building permits are issued, drawings and specifications are rushed out to subcontractors for bids. You hope to receive bids back in thirty days and start awarding contracts as fast as you can with no time to wait for another community's building permits to get issued. The goal of bidding on multiple communities at once always creates hassles and headaches. Or does it?

When you use unit pricing instead of lump-sum pricing, you can apply the same unit price to future jobs. For example, if you awarded a drywall contract to Dudley's Drywall for $0.33/SF for drywall material and $0.45/SF for labor and sundry materials, you could simply apply these rates to the next job. You may need to adjust for job-specific differences, like having more volume ceilings or curved walls, but most often, the same unit pricing will apply. As discussed earlier, this changes a thirty-day bid process into a five-minute phone call.

This strategy has always proved a big winner for me. I would tell the subcontractor, "If you can give me a good enough unit price, I'll give you the next two communities." I might have even negotiated one or two pennies per square foot less or gotten him to agree to hold pricing for a longer duration. Of course, we would field verify all the square footage quantities and adjust contracts based on those verified quantities. I would also take into account fluctuating material prices, as verified by independent sources, to be fair.

The drywall subcontractor and I agreed this was a win-win. Each community does not have to stand alone, nor do you have to go out to bid on all three communities at the same time; you simply start up the new community as it becomes ready. Because you've already negotiated pricing, contracts are written quicker, and construction starts sooner on the other communities in the pod.

Now that we have clustered a few communities together as a pod, we are ready to implement innovative supply chain solutions, right? Not so fast. For a variety of reasons, subcontractors end up with lots of different companies supplying materials to them. When you can align the upstream distributors and manufacturers in a cluster of communities, you have far more opportunities to take waste out of current material delivery methods. For example, if Dudley's Drywall is the selected subcontractor on one of your clusters and you have the same distributor too, you can enable more full truckloads of drywall to be delivered, dropping off to multiple locations within a small geographical area.

Drywall distributors use a variety of measurements to track their business performance. One of them is the *quantity of drywall per truckload*. When they frequently deliver half truckloads, more trucks and drivers are required to deliver the same amount of drywall. Yet the cluster brings an increased chance that more than one house will need drywall the same day, enabling more full truckload deliveries. Increasing a distributor's drywall sales without increasing their overhead costs makes them more profitable. Here's what I found: When the distributor's costs go down, they will often share those advantages with you in the form of lower prices. I have saved quite a lot of money doing just this.

The facilitation of the same distributor and manufacturer in this clustering method can prove tricky, however. An extenuating circumstance to watch out for is how you affect the subcontractor's buying power with his current suppliers. One time, I made a good deal with a distributor of roofing materials, one that offered great pricing, guaranteed supply when we needed it, and added customer service personnel to encourage smooth field operations. As soon as the deal was signed, we were off and running. The first order of business was to tell the roofing subcontractors about the deal and direct them to our new supplier for all the roofing needs in my region. But in this case, my favorite roofer did not use that supplier and had to open a new account with them. And now that they were buying a large quantity from this new supplier, they lost some buying power with the supplier they had been using for years. This win for us meant they would have to pay a slightly higher price for the work they did for other builders.

Subsequently, my roofer then became a little less competitive on all the other work they were bidding, a situation with the potential to hurt their business and possibly cause them to raise the labor and profit portion of their pricing to us.

If you find yourself in a similar situation and let it continue, it could erase some or all of the great benefits you just negotiated with your new distributor. So watch out for your subcontractors' current supplier relations. Don't be afraid to conduct confidential conversations with your most trusted subcontractors during your negotiations with a distributor or manufacturer. It's better to have their insight sooner rather than after the deal is signed.

Another facet to consider? Whiplash—a supply chain management term used to describe the effect of high and low swings of inventory on hand in response to shifts in customer demand. One month they are overstocked; the next they have empty shelves. This term can also apply to subcontractor labor management. Remember that whiteboard I was telling you about that I almost wiped clean by skimming the back of my jacket against it? The whiteboard's main purpose was to alert the managers of the number of crews needed on a certain day. On some days, they needed six crews; on other days, forty-two crews. But if they only have access to thirty crews, they must decide what to do on the days they need forty-two.

Podding communities together in a geographical location can affect efficiency in multiple ways, including the utilization of labor. The pods make it easier to keep one crew busy, preventing them from having to drive from one job site to the next in a single day. Nobody gets paid for windshield time.

FROM PLUMBER TO BUSINESSMAN

Most plumbers are in business because someone who was an excellent plumber decided to start his own business. Yet good plumbers are not necessarily great business people. This same issue applies to carpenters, tile setters, electricians, roofers, and every other trade it takes to build a house. Nearly all of them were first a tradesperson before becoming a business owner. Many do not have college degrees, let alone business management degrees. Many of them don't know if they are profitable until they do their taxes at the end of the year.

Subcontractors frequently base their pricing on the perception of their ability to create cash flow. When they operate more efficiently, they might gain a pricing advantage over a competitor. One of the homebuilding companies I worked for hired business consultants for our key subcontractors to help them become better business people.

I can't take any credit for this idea, but I can certainly attest to its benefit. It was argued that we were throwing money away, or that we were benefiting our competition because most of our subcontractors also worked for other builders. While there is some truth to this, I don't believe any builders benefited as much as we did.

The subcontractors we offered this service to were so thankful; their gratitude was exhibited in lower pricing, better customer service, and higher quality construction. They talked about what we did for them often, conveying high esteem for our company. We benefited from their loyalty for many years—an exceptional investment.

While we had no visibility into what took place—with the entire consultation remaining private between only the subcontractor and the business consultant—we paid for the initial service. We paid for a certain number of hours, and if the subcontractor wanted more services, they had the option to continue working with the consultant on their own. Some chose to continue, while others were satisfied with the training and coaching we funded.

The single most important concept to teach the subcontractor was the discipline of job costing. As homebuilders, we apply all our business costs to a particular house. Otherwise, we wouldn't know which homes were profitable and which were not. In most cases, the job cost data is used to set sales prices to ensure we make enough money on each house. Subcontractors are most successful when they know if they are making money on each home or not, providing the opportunity to analyze what happened when a house resulted in a loss. When you wait until the end of the year, the ability to analyze and learn from mistakes diminishes.

So many opportunities await to reduce construction costs; one book isn't enough to cover them all. Hopefully, the information here proves ample enough to get you thinking so you can begin to apply your own ideas. I like to imagine that all my subcontractors were employees and then consider if I would communicate with them, interact with them, and motivate them in the same way I do now. If the answer is *yes*, then I am probably fostering a culture that produces the best results.

Take a minute to review the communications that you recently sent to your subcontractors. How is the tone? Are your messages designed to uplift and motivate them to do better? To be better? When you require a face-to-face meeting, do you ever go to their office, or do you always make them come to yours?

Have you been to their office and met the staff responsible for building your homes?

Much of what I learned about subcontractor operations occurred on a job site or at their office. I learned very little about them in my office.

In addition to the value of what I learn, they appreciate it when you take an interest in their business. They appreciate it when you show that you care by spending time getting to know their team. Running a subcontracting business proves a huge undertaking, fraught with stress and worry. They are proud of what they have built and are eager to show it to someone who cares. More times than not, I was told I was the only builder who had ever visited their office. The commitment, loyalty, and priority service were returned to me and my company in the form of lower prices, higher quality work, higher levels of customer service, and extra work they would do for free. Above all, I built friendships that I could never have developed in a conference room.

It's easy to establish a culture of adversarial reciprocity between the homebuilder and subcontractor. Yet it takes a concerted effort to create a culture of mutual respect and encouragement. One culture is toxic and will cost you a great deal of money. The other is nurturing and fosters continual improvement for each side. Usually, only one makes you excited to get up and go to work in the morning.

FINAL THOUGHTS: THE TRADE COUNCIL

Working on a Wednesday night was often hailed as the highlight of my month for all of us. Especially for me. I know, that sounds crazy, but when you're talking about the Trade Council, all becomes clear.

A group of twelve selected subcontractors met once per month on a Wednesday night, assembling as a team to guide some of the decision making for our homebuilding company.

Each year they elected a president and a few other positions to lead the group. A few of us attended and contributed somewhat, but this group's strength lay in the way they interacted with each other in the Trade Council meetings and how this higher level of cooperation manifested on the job sites.

Every company celebrates when they achieve good communication among their employees; it's acclaimed as an amazing accomplishment. But when your suppliers communicate effectively, it brings your company to a whole new level of high performance. When reports of a defect in our houses surfaced, this group went to work solving it. Soon after, they drove performance to zero-defect homes.

Zero-defect homes, higher profit margins, highest quality, and the highest customer service scores were some of the results of the Trade Council's efforts. They became a permanent advisory group to our operations team and brought about the highest performance our company had ever known.

Becoming a member of the Trade Council was considered an honor. Each person took pride in being part of the team. They knew that their needs were important to us, that we cared about their success as well as our own. Our investment in hosting this group paid for itself over and over again. I cannot imagine a homebuilding company without a Trade Council.

The President of the Trade Council called the meeting to order, read the minutes from the last session, and started with the first item on the agenda. I was only a spectator there; the real heroes were the knights around the table. I took great satisfaction in the functionality of this group and that I didn't have to be in charge. I'll always fondly remember those Trade Council nights and the successes they achieved—they produced too many win-wins to count, but too many to forget. Those winning Wednesdays still bring a smile to my face.

PART III

Implementation

CHAPTER 8

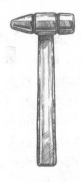

Which Tools Are Right for You Right Now?

I was feeling good about finally getting back into the gym after a thirteen-year hiatus. I had been anticipating this day for a long time. Later, I found myself at home after a strenuous workout, and something didn't feel right. The pain grew as the hours ticked by. Not the kind of pain that connotes an imminent increase in muscle, but the kind that makes you wonder what you might have done wrong.

I knew it had been a long time, but I was into super fitness and had trained with some of the best athletes in the country. Lifting weights, racing bicycles, and skiing were what I did after a long day on the job site as a carpenter and mason. Fitness was my middle name.

After I got married and we had children right away, my focus changed from being all about me to being all about them. It wasn't deliberate, but I didn't step foot in a gym or compete in 100-mile bike races again until the older children were big enough to start watching the younger ones.

No matter your fitness level, thirteen years is a long time to go without working out. I had seriously underestimated my new starting point and jumped right back into my old weightlifting routines. I started with lighter weights, or so I thought, and pushed myself hard so I could get back into shape fast.

I tore a ligament in my right elbow and stretched the same ligament in my left elbow, keeping me out of the gym for another year. One year later, I hired a trainer to help prevent me from hurting myself once more. She started by ensuring I use lighter weights until my body got used to exercising again. Each exercise has several levels of progression, and my trainer kept me at the basic level for longer than I would have done without her.

Each of the tools in this book also includes several levels of progression. Starting at the base level and moving up to higher levels of complexity should be done slowly and deliberately. This chapter is based on the discipline required for successful implementation, intended to prevent you from getting hurt by jumping in too hard, too fast.

ASSESS YOUR STARTING POINT

The first task of a fitness trainer is to assess your starting point. He or she will evaluate your balance, stability, strength, and stamina before prescribing an exercise program. A good trainer can quickly determine what levels of success you can achieve, knowing a bad start can set you back one year or worse.

I often get asked the same question about these methods to reduce construction costs: "How much money can I save by implementing all these supply chain solutions?" I always provide the same answer: "It depends on where you're starting from." I can tell you how much you should be paying for drywall, but unless you know how much you are currently paying, I have no way of telling how much money you can save.

Another question I'm often asked is, "What should I do first?" While an excellent question, I can't give an answer without knowing more about your construction operations, subcontractor base, distributors, and manufacturers. You want to start with strategies that will bring your team a win quickly and achieve enough cost savings to inspire a continuation of the opportunities.

Just as a person new to weightlifting should not attempt to squat with a 405-pound barbell, a builder should not try to implement a supply chain strategy in which they have no expertise or resources to reach success. After gaining an understanding of the different methods to reduce construction costs, assess your team's knowledge, skills, and experiences, and combined with the capability of your subcontractors and suppliers, you will know where to begin. Often, a distributor or manufacturer is the one who prompts the ideas you tackle first.

I have seen other builders attempt solutions similar to the ones in this book but only take part of my guidance to heart—and fail terribly. Once they discovered how much some of their materials should cost, they stopped the process and merely beat that new information over the head of their subcontractors and suppliers, attempting to compel them to provide lower prices. This method reaps minimal benefit, and all of it short-term. As the saying goes, *what goes around, comes around*, and subcontractors and suppliers that feel slighted and maligned will often get you back in the long run.

The supply chain strategies laid out in this book depend on the mutual cooperation of each company involved. Even in the cases where you eliminate an entity, do it with their full knowledge and support. Some of my most rewarding negotiations have emerged when I eliminated a distributor from a supply line—yet he acknowledged my goal and complimented me, thanked me for the way we communicated with him, and ended with each of us hoping our paths would cross again someday. This resulting scenario should illustrate your goal in every instance when someone in your supply lines loses your business upon the implementation of a new supply chain strategy. One of residential construction's most appealing attributes that makes it such a warm and gratifying industry is the long-term nature of our supplier relations. Once a friend, always a friend.

In residential construction, we build homes in the same market, with the same subcontractors and building material distributors, for decades. Your reputation as a trustworthy company takes many years to develop—and only one instance to destroy. Protect your reputation by treating others well, even when you're firing them.

WHICH MATERIALS SHOULD YOU CONSOLIDATE FIRST?

Discovering opportunities to consolidate distribution can get a little tricky. But once implemented, your strategy to consolidate distribution runs itself with little or no maintenance from you, the builder. And while the monthly or annual savings may appear relatively small, the consolidation keeps producing those savings year over year. It's an excellent long-term solution.

The idea of combining door hardware and light fixtures was made possible through our "box of locks" deal with the door hardware manufacturer. I made similar deals with two different manufacturers at two different times in my career. The first time, the manufacturer created a new assembly line just for our company, and the box of locks was assembled for each house by lot number and address. The second time, a different manufacturer had "pack to order" capabilities at one of their plants. Typically only a distributor's function, their ability to create a box of locks took us by surprise.

Each manufacturer made the effort to create the box of locks for us for at least two reasons: the volume of purchases we generated, and the maturity of our supply chain management team. Once we had the box-of-locks process in play—and thus cautiously watched the flow from manufacturing to the job site, as well as interviewed multiple companies to provide last-mile distribution—putting them on the same truck with light fixtures seemed somewhat elementary. For the rest of this story in detail, simply review Chapter Two.

One key point I didn't reveal in that chapter, however, rises pertinent now: We used more than one method to get the box of locks to the job site. Each of the methods we instigated worked well, some better than others. For example, we had some of the boxes delivered directly to the site via UPS. Yet we faced an obstacle when UPS discovered a big deficiency in delivering to a location that does not yet have an address. We also employed cross-docking services with several last-mile logistics companies, yet for some of them, finding and navigating through a construction site was not part of their skillset.

The lesson we learned? Use last-mile logistics services, such as subcontractors or distributors, who already serve our industry. They know how to service houses that do not yet appear on a map software application. Once you conquer that challenge, this strategy proves simple.

Other key opportunities lie in Active Adult communities, with their uniquely high volume, limited home-buyer choices, and production-driven schedule (as opposed to sales-driven). The production-driven schedule means house construction will continue despite sales pace. The schedule may adjust up or down at times, but not as erratically as a sales-driven schedule with its frequent starts and stops. In the community where we put floor tile and drywall on the same trucks, the home buyer had only four choices of tile color with no options on the quantity or area where the tile could be installed.

The limited number of choices and high volume made it simple to calculate a three-week buffer of inventory at the drywall distributor's warehouse (which I rented for a meager price), ensuring a steady, uninterrupted flow of material to the job site. If we had attempted this strategy of uninterrupted inventory flow on a traditional housing community, where the home buyer is allowed to choose from thousands of different tiles and apply them anywhere in the house they desire, this level of complexity would have made it impossible—and definitely unprofitable.

Keep your eye out for communities with materials consistent from one house to the next, and you'll find conditions favorable for reducing the cost of construction operations by reducing the number of tire tracks on the job site.

When to Buy Direct and When Not To

When I proposed buying materials directly from distributors or manufacturers and I encountered fear in the eyes of my managers, I was puzzled. You see, in the 1970s I purchased all my own materials. Then again in the 1980s while in the military, I requisitioned all materials needed for a job site. Now, in the 1990s, buying directly struck fear in my bosses' hearts. *Really weird*, I thought.

But once you understand how the production home-building system works, you realize it's not so weird. We have essentially become management companies, no longer construction companies, because now everything is subcontracted with a labor and materials turn-key contract. In fact, the system we have grown so accustomed to boasts many advantages—and harbors many disadvantages, too. One of the benefits lies in who takes responsibility for any materials on the job site that are stolen, wasted, or mismanaged. Not the homebuilder.

And one big disadvantage sticks out like a pink elephant in the room: We sometimes pay too much for building materials.

Most homebuilders procure a small amount of materials directly. Most likely, the motivation for doing so is to save money. So why not buy a few more materials and save some more money? Your response might entail a list of added responsibilities: ordering and receiving the materials when they arrive at the job site, possibly providing a signature for the delivery, staging them so no one has to move them twice, watching that they don't get stolen or abused, getting them into the hands of the installer, and finally, approving the invoice for payment.

Wow, what a good response to my proposition. Sounds prudent at first glance. But a simple answer to all these obstacles is at hand.

Have the installer order, receive, and store the materials for you. Once they're installed, you can approve the invoice for payment.

But now you may be wondering something else: If you pay a subcontractor to do everything he was doing before you removed the materials from his turn-key contract, and you're paying for the materials, what is the benefit of buying directly?

In each case when I decided to buy direct, I procured the materials at a low price and paid the subcontractor a small fee to manage them. The fee I paid the subcontractor was substantially smaller than the mark-up he was putting on the materials. And yes, it proved financially beneficial every time.

The products you decide to procure directly will depend on your operation team's core competencies, their knowledge and understanding of certain products, and the relationships you have with distributors and manufacturers. My decision to buy roof trusses and have my framer order, receive, and install them was due to an excellent negotiation with the roof truss company and a willing framer. The framer and the truss company initially suggested it; all I did was listen and act on it.

My decision to buy roof tile directly was enabled by a massive strategic sourcing deal negotiated by the corporate home office and further negotiated as a direct buy deal by me locally. In this particular case, we had a favored roofing subcontractor that had limited resources to grow his business at a time when we were rapidly expanding. Our procurement of roof tile increased his production capacity. A win-win ensued.

Each time we decided to procure building materials directly, the opportunity seemed to fall into our lap. We did not go out looking for opportunities to buy stuff, we just listened for cues where it could work. Once we started doing it and reaped the benefit of lower costs, we kept an open mind to more opportunities. If you do it right, and the installer does the ordering, receiving, and on-site management (for a fair fee), you can make a great deal of money with this strategy to lower construction costs.

WHICH KITS TO START WITH

I did not set out to create kits of materials that distributors assembled and dropped off at the job site. We simply engaged our distributors in our efforts to reduce the cost of building a house, and one by one, ideas emerged. It helps for you to meet all your distributors. They often have ideas not being implemented on your job sites because your subcontractors are not interested. So get to know your distributors. They possess vast knowledge of the products they carry, and the process their customers use to procure and install them. They're good people to know.

If your subcontractor in a specific product category frequently changes distributors based on pricing or availability, you might have already spotted opportunities for improvement. You can solve availability issues by giving the distributor SKU and Date Needed data for future orders. And pricing is negotiable. Sometimes the volume and promise to fast-pay a distributor can achieve lower pricing than the subcontractor was getting. And here's a tip: *do not underestimate fast-pay.* I spend a great deal of time with distributors, and most of them figure they spend 40 to

60 percent of their time as a bill collector. They have trouble getting paid on time, so builders can entice a distributor to do things differently just on the promise of fast-pay. Some of the homebuilders I worked for offered ten-day pay—enough to make most distributors drool.

There is an incremental degradation of sophistication as you move down the supply chain from manufacturers to subcontractors. So the further upstream you can push a task, the more efficiently it will get accomplished. Explore kitting with your distributors, and get them to think about the products they carry, as well as the products they do not yet sell.

Kitting does not always mean you will buy the products directly. You could engineer the solution and have the subcontractor purchase the kits as part of their normal material procurement process. But when you do this, you have to be careful to get the full benefit of the kit by taking a simple step: *Know precisely what the difference in cost was and apply it as a deduction to your subcontract agreement.*

A subcontractor may fail to see the benefit of having kits made up for them. That's okay. Have them implement the kits anyhow, and see if they change their mind over time. Companies that have never implemented a continual improvement program might lack vision seeing the efficiencies kitting can provide. Also, stay open to accepting that, sometimes, your kits may not prove as beneficial as hoped. But don't stop trying.

HOW TO SEND THE RIGHT DEMAND SIGNALS

Sending desired future consumption information through the supply chain has the single most significant potential to lower construction costs than any other cost-saving strategy you will employ. Our distributors and manufacturers are desperate to have detailed SKU and Date Needed data—thirty days, sixty days, or ninety days ahead of time—to optimize operations. Today, they have to guess what every homebuilder plans to order—and when they will order them. Thus the truth remains: They always guess incorrectly, and homebuilders pay for that inefficiency in the form of higher prices.

Also note this: Sending proper demand signals through the supply chain does not compel a *quick* win for a homebuilder looking to lower costs fast. But it's the *most significant* win, with the longest-term sustainability, and therefore, the most critical operations scheme you will develop. As with each of the supply chain management methods published in this book, sending proper demand signals starts with converting lump-sum pricing into unit pricing. The process of detailing your construction contracts with the proper SKU, quantity needed, and pricing means you have already completed 75 percent of your project to send effective demand signals.

The management of SKU data is best done in your company's back-office system used for accounting. Yet today, most builders are still utilizing the lump-sum functionality of their back-office system and may need to do some program customization to enable the management of SKU data. Then your back-office system will look more like manufacturing than homebuilding, empowering every method described in this book.

The next step required to marry SKU data with Date Needed information is correlating construction schedule activities with purchase orders. Use a system that can coordinate data with your back-office system, or employ a third-party system that can combine the data and send it to the various supply chain entities.

As I mentioned earlier, one way to send SKU and Date Needed data is to create a zero-dollar purchase order containing the SKUs appropriate to an entity's operations. Zero-dollar purchase orders can be distributed electronically when your back-office system starts up a new house. Another method lies in creating reports from your back-office system that can be sent electronically and absorbed into a distributor's Warehouse Management System and a manufacturer's Material Requirements Planning system (MRP).

I consider the development of automated SKU and Date Needed data as one of my most gratifying career accomplishments. It took a great deal of work from our IT department, as well as from the operations and IT departments of the manufacturers and distributors we initially partnered with, to make this system work. When people and systems are pushed beyond their individual abilities and together in robust collaboration achieve something great as a team, a special bond is formed. Creating computer-to-computer communication, with no humans involved, not only lowered our pricing but increased the margins of both the manufacturer and distributor—a win-win-win. Triple kudos all around. I love when that happens.

ASKING SUBCONTRACTORS THE RIGHT QUESTIONS

No matter how long you've been working with the same subcontractors, you can always find opportunity to improve. We helped our subcontractors lower their operating costs in at least three ways: by making changes to schedules, by modifying our communication methods when changes occurred, and by evaluating what products we chose to use on our houses. All this forged a stronger bond between our two companies, resulting in lower prices for labor and materials. Unfortunately, longstanding working relationships can sometimes prove a hindrance to progress. Because you've worked together so long, each party makes assumptions about what the other is thinking, preventing both from communicating the pain points or circumstances holding back lower prices.

The key to visualizing opportunities for improvement lies in pretending that the workers in the field are your employees. This perspective permits you to be more sensitive to making changes in the construction schedule, allowing late-stage customization from the home buyer, ensuring the job is ready before they begin their work. Build collaboration by asking the right questions and then acting on them to make improvements to their experience on your job site. When your subcontractors know their needs are important to you, they will give you a competitive advantage—with the best crews and best pricing.

As I mentioned earlier, start by asking, "What is it we do that costs you money?" Listen carefully to what they tell you, ask clarifying questions, and then act on solutions to eliminate the barriers. The first time you ask, they will give a general, low-risk answer. As they see you working on their concerns, they will open up with more specific pain points. Be careful not to turn their concerns around and blame them for the circumstances. They want to know they can trust you with the information they give you. As trust grows, so will the quality of information they provide.

Although they were few, I did have some subcontractors that wanted nothing to do with any of my continual improvement processes and were content with business "as is." That's okay. Look for other subcontractors willing to explore opportunities with you, and slowly wean your company away from the folks not interested in striving for higher efficiency. In my experience, about 5 percent of my contractors did not want to participate in my supply chain solution endeavors.

Refining and honing the subcontractor's operations entails an ongoing effort of continual improvement. Just because you asked them about *what we do that costs you money* last year, doesn't mean that asking again this year will produce the same answer. The changes you made as a result of your conversations with a subcontractor will change their perspective. Ask the same question again, and you'll get a new answer. Show that you welcome their continued sharing of concerns so you know what to work on, and your bond will continually strengthen. Lower prices will follow, whether driven by the lower cost of doing business or lower margins due to your stronger bond.

REGIONAL DIFFERENCES

To make these supply chain management methods more natural to understand, I purposely omitted from the previous chapters the regional differences that can dramatically affect pricing. Because our industry is so fragmented and localized, it is difficult to generalize things like construction operations, subcontractor and builder relations, and labor pricing. Attempting to cover all the nuances of our industry in the many markets we build homes would have made these concepts much harder to understand. This section is a brief look at what makes us different from one location to another. Like most aspects involving labor, prices are lowest in the Southern states and highest in the big cities along both coasts. The starting point I referred to at the beginning of this chapter will vary from one homebuilder to another in the same market and also vary within the same homebuilding company from one market to another.

And then there's Texas.

One day, just after finishing the negotiation on a stone veneer product, I called the purchasing manager in each of our eighteen divisions to tell them the good news: "We're getting stone for $3.00 per square foot." Each of the managers were thrilled; their house costs were about to go down. Then I called my purchasing manager in Dallas. With exuberance, I told him about the deal, and he started laughing. That was not the response I'd received from any of the other purchasing managers.

I was puzzled. "What's so funny?" I asked.

He said, "Ken, I get natural stone delivered to the site—and installed on the wall—for $3.00 per square foot."

Wow. I removed Texas from my exclusive deal with this stone veneer manufacturer.

Texas is a unique market compared to the rest of the United States. In most cases, Texas homebuilders buy their own materials and hire labor-only subcontractors to install them. Texans subcontract only about five or six categories as a turn-key operation. In the remaining categories, Texas builders know precisely *how much the milk is* because they buy the products directly from distributors and a few manufacturers. Nonetheless, all the supply chain solutions described in these chapters still apply to Texas; they're just starting from a different place than builders in other regions.

In the Northeast, it's common for a builder to buy bricks and hire a mason to install them. From market to market, some differences change the starting point of supply chain management techniques, but not the strategy itself. And, as I mentioned earlier, the starting point provides the missing piece to easily answer the question, *How much money can be saved by implementing all these strategies?* Notably, labor costs primarily drive regional differences; materials do not fluctuate as much from region to region.

Regional labor costs are driven by the area's cost of living. A living wage for a carpenter in Kansas City is much different than if he were performing the same tasks in San Francisco. Supply and demand also play a part. If an area has more demand for carpenters than people to fill those jobs, the labor rate goes up. Fuel prices also play into costs when much driving is required. Taxation rates also affect wages, giving places like Texas, with no state income taxes, an advantage over high-tax states.

Governmental regulations distinguish one market from another in a myriad of ways: in the requirements to entitle land and subdivide plats, in the building department's willingness to support development, in coastal commission and engineering impact reviews, in building requirements in fire prone areas, and on and on. The government can add a lot to the cost of building a home.

Some workers are paid an hourly rate; some are piece workers. Piece workers get paid a flat labor rate per unit of material installed. I know a guy who installs roof sheathing and gets paid by the square foot of sheathing he installs; he makes more money than most college graduates. Workers favor piece work, which is most common in the Southwestern states, because they can dictate how much money they make. If they want to make more money, they install more material. It's an efficient way to pay a construction worker. In the Northeastern states, the hourly wage rules the day.

When I look at my own family, especially the temperaments of my five children, I can perhaps paint a picture of what opportunities and situations may lie ahead for them. Raising five children who are only six years apart in age, my wife and I felt we wanted to instill them with some helpful life skills from the get-go. Until self-discipline takes shape, parental discipline is necessary to prevent children from veering onto dangerous paths. Yet we saw growth in our children's hearts and characters only through the use of discipline methods that spoke to their unique temperaments. For example, while grounding a child to their room for a period of time was effective for four of our children, one was happy to stay in his room and play, color, read, and daydream. While offering a bonus on their allowance for good grades was motivating for three of them, the other two were not impressed.

Yes, kids are entirely different from one another, and so are the markets where we build homes. On more than one occasion, I've made the mistake of not recognizing regional differences and tried to implement a one-size-fits-all approach to supply chain management. Here's the takeaway: Perform your due diligence in each market before you pull the trigger on a big deal, and you'll avoid the laughing voice of a purchasing manager telling you, "Your deal is no good here."

CHAPTER 9

For a Quick Win

O ver the years whenever I introduced homebuilders to supply chain management methods to control construction costs, they frequently requested a cautionary approach: "Implement a 'pilot program' first," they would say, "just to prove the methods work." Then a phased roll-out could follow.

Though I've utilized these methods for years in multiple markets, each homebuilding leader believes their division and market are unique, so a limited-exposure test period often appeals to them.

So just as a matter of survival as a supply chain manager, I learned to produce quick wins.

However, "quick" is not the adjective I would link to any supply chain management protocol. As these strategies appear so different from our industry's conventional methods, they can seem strange at first. Yet once you get past the pilot program and realize the benefits and enrichment to your construction process, the thought of reverting back to the old methods of controlling costs will trouble you. Until then, though, quick wins are essential to get key players on board.

This chapter gives you a practical collection of quick wins that you can apply to your own situation; the first I'll describe in detail and the rest in summary form.

Before we get started with the detailed process of a quick win, however, I'd like to once again stress the need for conversion from lump-sum pricing to unit pricing. Everything hinges on this objective. Whether you manage unit pricing in your back-office accounting software or on spreadsheets, it must be done. Undoubtedly, managing unit pricing in your accounting software is preferable, enhancing your ability to run reports on historical cost data. However, even if you have to track unit pricing on spreadsheets until you can make programming changes to your back-office system, it's better than nothing. While perhaps a great deal of extra work, the results are still worth it.

DRYWALL CONTRACTING BEST PRACTICES

You've probably noticed that I like to use drywall for demonstrating how to apply supply chain management methods to production homebuilding. Drywall is a significant spend category with few SKUs, and it's simple to count the quantity delivered to the house and measure the quantity installed. We will use the drywall category again for the demonstration of a quick win. Here's the process:

- Choose one community, preferably one with popular floor plans so you can apply the benefits as widely as possible from this single activity.
- Obtain the lump-sum drywall contract prices for each floor plan type.

o Kenton, 2,623 SF house, $7,895

o Kenwick, 3,300 SF house, $11,200

o Kennington, 3,620 SF house, $12,050

- Measure the walls and ceilings of an inventory house where drywall was already installed. If an inventory house is unavailable, you may have to use a model home; just be careful not to get it dirty (the sales lady will not be happy with you).

    o Create a spreadsheet in portrait orientation with the following headings:

        ▪ Community, Lot No., Floor Plan, Date

Community: **Pinto Estates** Lot **72**	Drywall Field Measurement					
Floor Plan: **Kenton** 2,623 SF						
Date: 5/18/2019	All measurements are in "inches"					
Room	**Length**	**Height**	**X**	**1/2"**	**5/8"**	**Water bd**
Entry	76	108	2	X	x	
Entry	52	108	2	X		
Entry window	12	4	2	X		
Entry window	60	4	2	X		
Entry window	12	4	2	X		
Entry window	60	4	2	X		
Entry ceiling	76	52			X	
Entry door	-36	96		X		
Entry window	-12	60	2	X		
Entry opening	-65	96		X		
Bed 3 Hallway	172	108		X		
Bed 3 Hallway	72	108		X		

FIGURE 10 DRYWALL FIELD MEASUREMENT WORKSHEET

    o Add the following column headings to your spreadsheet. This becomes the worksheet you will take to the field to record the measurements of all the walls and ceilings.

        ▪ Room, Length, Height, multiplier, ½", 5/8", Water Board

    o If you suspect an error in the measurements during the data entry stage, the Room name will help you find the mistake and correct it before moving on. The Room name also helps keep track of what you have measured, saving you from measuring the same room twice.

- o The Length of the wall is measured at the bottom of the wall, from corner to corner. If the wall is segmented in several planes, measure them each as separate walls.
- o The ceiling Height is typically the same from room to room, and ditto marks can be used to speed up the recording process.
  - Sometimes the ceiling height is the same on the entire floor level. Sometimes it's the same throughout the whole house.
- o Don't forget to record the ceiling measurement; it will be a combination of some of the walls you already measured.
- o Walls are typically ½" thick drywall, except the house/garage wall, which is 5/8" thick.
  - When you measure the walls, designate the drywall thickness on the worksheet.
- o Ceilings are typically 5/8" drywall.
  - Designate them as 5/8" on the worksheet.
- o Wet areas where ceramic tile will be installed in bath and shower locations often use some kind of water-resistant board.
  - Designate these walls as Water Board, or Water Bd, on the worksheet.
- o Garage walls and ceilings are typically 5/8".
  - Designate 5/8" for the garage walls and ceilings on the worksheet.
- One person does the measuring, and the other does the recording. I recommend using a pencil so you can make quick corrections and still keep the entries neat.
  - o With two people, a 3,400 SF house takes about 45 minutes to measure and record.

- Deduct all doors and window openings by using a minus sign to represent negative numbers. To mitigate mistakes during data entry on the computer, make sure the minus signs are easy to read on your worksheet.

- When two walls are the same size, use the multiplier column to show how many there are. This is convenient for doors and windows that are the same size, too.

- Add the 4" or so window surrounds, too. Enter the width in the Height column.

- All measurements are made in inches. It's too confusing to use feet and inches, and mistakes sometimes occur in measuring, recording, and data entry. Keep everything in inches. Round to the nearest inch.

- I like to start with the first floor, the first room on the left, and work in a clockwise direction, room by room, around the house. No matter what pattern you use to navigate around the house, it's best to stick with the same pattern every time. It will save time and limit mistakes.

- Enter all the measurements into your computer, and create a sum total for each material. I modified my spreadsheet to do this automatically, controlled by which column I put the "X" in.

- Now that you have the total square inches of drywall required to complete each plan type, convert to square feet by dividing the total number of square inches by 144.

Community: **Pinto Estates**			Drywall Field Measurement			
Floor Plan: **Kenton**		2,623 SF				
Date: **5/18/2019**			All measurements are in "inches"			
Room	Length	Height	X	1/2"	5/8"	Water bd
Entry	76	108	2	X	x	
Entry	52	108	2	X		
Entry window	12	4	2	X		
Entry window	60	4	2	X		

2 Car Garage	24	108	2		X	
2 Car Garage ceiling	24	43			X	
2 Car Garage self clo door	-32	80			X	
2 Car Garage out door	-32	80			X	
2 Car Garage G. door	-192	84			X	

1/2" Drywall	6017	SF
5/8" Drywall	3959	SF
Water Board	169	SF

FIGURE 11 TOP AND BOTTOM OF DRYWALL FIELD MEASUREMENT WORKSHEET

- This total is the exact amount of drywall installed on the walls and ceilings. Your totals should look something like this.

Kenton	Delivered	Field Measured	Waste
1/2" Drywall		6017 SF	
5/8" Drywall		3959 SF	
Water Board		169 SF	

Kenwick	Delivered	Field Measured	Waste
1/2" Drywall		6653 SF	
5/8" Drywall		4880 SF	
Water Board		140 SF	

Kennington	Delivered	Field Measured	Waste
1/2" Drywall		7222 SF	
5/8" Drywall		5200 SF	
Water Board		140 SF	

FIGURE 12 FIELD VERIFIED DRYWALL QUANTITY COMPARISON

- Obtain the amount of drywall that was delivered and stocked in each plan type. You may have to wait until another of each plan type gets built. Have your superintendent count the sheets stocked in one of each floor plan, or have him alert you when the house is stocked, and you can go out and count them. These days, most drywallers are using 4'x10' sheets, but it depends on the house. When you are counting sheets, be sure to take note of the size and thickness of the sheets. Your stocked drywall quantities should look something like this.

Kenton	Delivered	Field Measured	Waste
1/2" Drywall	7000 SF		
5/8" Drywall	4400 SF		
Water Board	192 SF		

Kenwick	Delivered	Field Measured	Waste
1/2" Drywall	7400 SF		
5/8" Drywall	5400 SF		
Water Board	180 SF		

Kennington	Delivered	Field Measured	Waste
1/2" Drywall	8160 SF		
5/8" Drywall	5880 SF		
Water Board	180 SF		

FIGURE 13 FIELD VERIFIED DRYWALL DELIVERY QUANTITY COMPARISON

- Divide the actual installed quantity from the stocked drywall quantity to arrive at the waste factor. A fair waste factor for most houses is 9 percent. In times of high demand, less skilled drywall crews waste more drywall than experienced crews. Let's take a look at the waste factor on these houses.

Kenton	Delivered	Field Measured	Waste
1/2" Drywall	7000 SF	6017 SF	14.0%
5/8" Drywall	4400 SF	3959 SF	10.0%
Water Board	192 SF	169 SF	12%

Kenwick	Delivered	Field Measured	Waste
1/2" Drywall	7400 SF	6653 SF	10.0%
5/8" Drywall	5400 SF	4880 SF	10.0%
Water Board	180 SF	140 SF	23%

Kennington	Delivered	Field Measured	Waste
1/2" Drywall	8160 SF	7222 SF	11.5%
5/8" Drywall	5880 SF	5200 SF	11.5%
Water Board	180 SF	140 SF	23%

FIGURE 14 FIELD VERIFIED DRYWALL WASTE FACTOR COMPARISON

- These floor plans, with actual drywall quantity plus 9 percent waste, should cost less than the current contracts reflect. Drywall costs per square foot of drywall (NOT the house's square feet of living space) are as follows:
  - ½" drywall@$0.243/SF + $0.02/SF stocking fee = $0.263/SF
  - 5/8" drywall@$0.273/SF + $0.02/SF stocking fee = $0.293/SF
  - ½" water resistant drywall@$0.32/SF + $0.02/SF stocking fee = $0.34/SF
- Drywall labor and sundry materials (corner bead, joint tape, joint compound, nails, screws, caulking) vary from region to region and city to city. For this exercise, we are going to use $0.40/SF for our labor price.
- Apply the labor and material pricing to the actual drywall quantities plus 9 percent waste to arrive at the fair price for labor and materials.

Kenton	Field Measured	add 9%	Mat'l & Labor	Fair Price
1/2" Drywall	6017	6559	$ 0.663	$ 4,348
5/8" Drywall	3959	4315	$ 0.693	$ 2,991
Water Board	169	184	$ 0.740	$ 136

Kenwick	Field Measured	add 9%	Mat'l & Labor	Fair Price
1/2" Drywall	6653	7252	$ 0.663	$ 4,808
5/8" Drywall	4880	5319	$ 0.693	$ 3,686
Water Board	180	196	$ 0.740	$ 145

Kennington	Field Measured	add 9%	Mat'l & Labor	Fair Price
1/2" Drywall	7222	7872	$ 0.663	$ 5,219
5/8" Drywall	5200	5668	$ 0.693	$ 3,928
Water Board	180	196	$ 0.740	$ 145

FIGURE 15 DRYWALL FAIR PRICING

- Now compare the old total contract prices to the new pricing to see how much savings you will achieve.

	Old	New	Adjustment
Kenton	$ 7,895	$ 7,475	$ 420
Kenwick	$ 11,200	$ 8,639	$ 2,561
Kennington	$ 12,050	$ 9,292	$ 2,758

FIGURE 16 DRYWALL CONRACT ADJUSTMENT BASED ON FIELD VERIFIED DRYWALL QUANTITIES

- As you can see, the Kenton floor plan was priced pretty close to what it should have been. The Kenwick and Kennington plans are way off. Next, approach your drywall subcontractor, ask him if the unit pricing for labor and materials is fair. If not, explore it together to find common ground. The Producer Price Index gets you in the ballpark on drywall material pricing, but local nuances always affect the price up or down. Ask him to show you invoices from his distributor to see his current pricing. Once you agree on unit pricing for material and labor, ask him to review your quantities, and see if he thinks they are fair. Explain the process for measuring the walls and ceilings and adding 9 percent.

I have repeated this process many times in many cities over several years, and each occurrence produced a similar result—a host of benefits that energized the entire homebuilding team:

✓ The homebuilder's costs on drywall labor and material were reduced, sometimes by a few hundred dollars—and sometimes by several thousand dollars per house.

✓ The homebuilder's purchasing department gained confidence in their ability to manage unit pricing, eagerly brainstorming ideas on what they could tackle next.

✓ The purchasing department may have been introduced to the drywall distributor, giving them an added resource for drywall supply chain concerns in the future.

✓ Equipped with a unit-price model for contracting drywall, the purchasing team changed the bidding process from thirty days to a five-minute phone call, accelerating the start of construction on a new community.

✓ When searching for new land to develop, a more accurate estimate could be made for the drywall portion of the direct costs when determining the feasibility of a land purchase.

✓ And best of all, the purchasing and construction personnel learned how to engage with subcontractors in a more meaningful way.

It's essential to use this new information in the right way. Your subcontractors are the folks who are building your houses and, as I mentioned earlier, will give you a competitive advantage with their best crews and best pricing when they know their needs are important to you. Use the unit pricing exercise above to bring you closer to your subcontractor, not drive a wedge between you. Subcontractors have pain points with suppliers that they usually don't tell homebuilders about. A homebuilder, especially a high-volume builder, can add clout to a small subcontractor, helping him get more favorable pricing or, in a constrained market, guaranteed supply from his distributor. Use this opportunity to work together to achieve more than you could in the three-bid environment, and your benefits will continue to grow.

DRYWALL PROCUREMENT – QUICK WIN

The first time I used this process—calculating drywall quantities and applying them to unit pricing to determine new contract amounts—I spent some time exploring this idea with several drywall distributors. I discovered that they each had an employee whose full-time job was to drive around the county and check to see which houses were ready to stock. Until that moment, I had assumed the subcontractors were calling them and arranging the deliveries when the job was ready. But not so.

Each drywall distributor had the same justification for hiring a full-time employee who drove from job to job all day long. It went something like this:

Frequently, when subcontractors called us to make a delivery, we'd discover that when the truck arrived, the job wasn't ready, causing us to turn around and go back to the yard. Those mistakes cost us so much money that we decided it's cheaper to have someone drive around all day and check the job sites.

How does this revelation change the scenario? I was content to pay the drywall subcontractor a fee to manage the delivery of drywall. Once I discovered they weren't managing the delivery at all, I was further compelled to buy direct from the distributor. I was also wondering who was paying for that guy to drive around the county.

When deciding to buy materials directly, one key challenge quickly arises: determining how they get ordered. Material lead time requirements often change based on a distributor's workload and upstream material supply, so having a built-in trigger to activate the order—such as an automated message generated from the scheduling software—can prove problematic. When buying directly, you want a process that works perfectly, every time, and having the distributor constantly checking your jobs for you is ideal. When I heard they were doing this, I wondered why I needed the subcontractor for the procurement of drywall. This realization then led me to my first purchase of drywall directly from a distributor.

If a subcontractor is providing a value-added service in the procurement of materials, they deserve to be compensated for it. I don't have any problem paying a subcontractor a markup on materials to solve a challenge I cannot remedy on my own at a lower cost. Whether the challenge is ordering, receiving, storage, prefabrication of multiple products, or theft prevention, I value the services our subcontractors perform. In this case, however, the value of their service was not worth the markup I was paying. Savings from buying drywall directly ranged from $450 to $1,100 per house.

Each time I procured drywall, I rewarded the subcontractor (the one that obliged my new builder-supplied material process) with more work. I gave them more contracts, increasing their overall revenue and relieving them of the additional credit extension needed to supply the additional work. In the right circumstances, this revenue-enhancer can increase his production capacity by allowing him to use his cash flow on managing crews instead of tying it up with suppliers. As I mentioned earlier, your best subcontractors will work with you to assuage 99 percent of the risk in managing builder-supplied materials when they know your heart is in the right place—wanting to help them as much as helping yourself, while enabling more people to buy a home, keeping us all in business for another day.

A Quick Win Through Consolidating Distribution

Consolidating distribution to reduce the tire tracks at your houses (the number of trucks delivering materials) proves an excellent way to reduce costs. If you engage your imagination, you can discover an unlimited array of potential solutions. For homes in the Southwestern US, one of the simplest combinations entails drywall and stucco materials. Many distributors in this region already carry both. The reason they don't get delivered on the same truck is because the two subcontractors—one working with drywall and the other stucco—don't collaborate with each other on material purchases. Only the homebuilder can facilitate this kind of consolidation. When combining the procurement of stucco, cement, lath wire, building paper, and drywall, I saved between $1,100 and $1,300 per house. Part of this savings was due to a direct buy on drywall and a private label deal on stucco.

Another combination most likely to work on your communities is light fixtures and finish electrical parts. In some parts of the country, these are already delivered on the same truck; in others, they are separate. For those markets procuring light fixtures from a different distributor than the finish electrical parts, don't forget the value-added services your light fixture supplier is performing for you, like adding the right length of chain for a hanging fixture or including light bulbs. Your electrical distributor can do this, too; just don't forget to include these services when evaluating costs. This quick and easy solution can save you $75 to $125 per house.

After the Honeymoon

Once you get your quick wins chalked up and pilot programs completed, celebrations may ensue, but it's not time to stop and just admire your successes. Keep in hot pursuit of excellence in your supply chain management strategies. As you do and you continue to apply this book's information, know this: Patience is required. Unless an organization remains relentless and willing to endure, their resolve could teeter on the edge of collapse as people revert back to old habits.

CHAPTER 10

How to Make Cost Reductions Sustainable

Another meeting was set to begin, and in the minutes beforehand, I sat chatting with Gary, seated next to me. Six months had passed since I'd last seen him, and I was curious how things were going. *Certainly, his response will be overwhelmingly positive*, I thought. We were both members of the Supply Chain Benchmark Group, made up of the purchasing or supply chain VPs of the top twenty homebuilding companies. While not all participated, all were invited. Our focus was set on creating solutions that raised the bar for supply chain methodology in the homebuilding industry without compromising our personal responsibility to ethics standards.

About a year before this event, I had shown Gary, who worked for another homebuilding company, how to implement a successful unit-pricing strategy, including all the details required for success. He was wary of the potential negative response from his management team, so I suggested he run a pilot program in one market, and then broadcast the results. He agreed.

When I saw him at the next Benchmark meeting six months later, he was excited to tell me about the pilot program's successes—how much money they saved, how easy it was to implement, and plans to expand the process. He could hardly contain himself, he was so excited.

Now, another six months after that encounter, I was talking with Gary again, and seated beside him, I could see from the look on his face he was hoping I wouldn't ask about the pilot. Surprised to see his grim demeaner, my curiosity and concern spilled over. When I asked him what happened, he said, "It completely fell apart."

I wondered how he could have implemented a supply chain strategy in a pilot program that netted excellent cost savings, yet then, six months later, it had all disintegrated. Lower direct costs mean higher profit margins—isn't that something his company was seeking? Large homebuilding companies in the US are run by educated businesspeople, so I was very surprised at this outcome.

His explanation proved profound. To implement the strategy, he said they had to find a different subcontractor because their current one wasn't willing to operate under this new method. That's okay—sometimes they do, and sometimes they don't.

Still, the new subcontractor worked out great, and construction costs went down. After a while, though, the operations team informed my friend that it wasn't working out the way they wanted, so they reverted to the old way with the prior subcontractor. The only explanation he could pull from them was that they "weren't comfortable" with the new method. Neither my friend nor I can define the word "comfortable" in the context here. What did they mean?

It took some time for Gary to put the puzzle together, one piece at a time, first from one person, and then another. He said they used phrases like, "That's just not who we are," "We don't operate like that," and "We like our old subcontractor." Then it occurred to me: This new, innovative strategy was not aligned with their company culture. To sustain changes in the new way the purchasing and construction departments operated, they needed a culture capable of supporting it.

This new understanding forms the basis of this chapter. To sustain the changes borne from a new supply chain strategy, the company culture may need to change with it.

A CULTURE TO SUPPORT THE NEW SUPPLY CHAIN

When ten people in a room hold up identical tuning forks and one person strikes theirs against a table, the other tuning forks will begin to vibrate and create a uniform tone. Similarly, the culture of a company sets the tone for what is and is not acceptable— behavior, beliefs, thinking, and feelings. When someone acts in a way unaligned with company culture, whether good or bad, the culture will emit an uncomfortable resonant frequency, deterring the behavior from occurring again. When employee behavior stays in alignment with company culture, they all emit the same pleasant tone.

The opening story about my Benchmark friend is true. What I didn't tell you is that a similar scenario happened with several other companies, too. Their stories run so parallel that I only need to mention one to represent other homebuilders who also tried this strategy and failed. In each case, the construction superintendents were happy with the changes, and senior managers were pleased with the money saved. You might think that would be enough to sustain a new process in your company. What else do you need? Well, a few things may need adjustment to sustain new methods of building houses.

Consider the technique a homebuilding company uses to teach its sales staff how to talk to customers. They hire consultants, go to seminars, read books, and roleplay with each other until they get it right. How does that compare to the way you talk to your subcontractors? Often, our communications with subcontractors are simply transactional in nature, rarely more. In many cases, only electronic communication is used; no one talks to real people anymore. Their contracts and change orders are emailed to them, and they simply sign and send them back. The construction schedule is electronic; the superintendent doesn't have to call them unless an exceptional circumstance occurs. In a sense, we don't treat subcontractors as real people who may respond best to some one-on-one attention and personal communication.

My experience over the years has led me to conclude that most supply chain solutions, especially methods that significantly lower construction costs, require the homebuilder to care more about other entities in the supply chain than they typically have in the past. Today, your communication with subcontractors is simply transactional; tomorrow, I hope it will encompass more—a caring attitude based on concern for their success and livelihood. In each touchpoint with subcontractors, show that you value them. I would even recommend roleplaying with the sales team as training for construction and purchasing departments. When subcontractors and suppliers feel like you care and a mutual emotional commitment begins to form, you will win their loyalty and create a culture that can sustain new methods of contracting for labor and materials.

Countless numbers of books, seminars, and consultants are available to help you build or change corporate culture. This section is not meant to replicate the solutions so aptly provided by those talented folks but instead, to offer my observations about specific characteristics of a homebuilding company's culture that are essential to the sustaining of a robust supply chain management program.

IT'S OKAY TO FAIL

I have never faulted a staff member for failing. I'm one of those people that believes if you're not failing once in a while, you're not trying hard enough to innovate. But if you don't learn a lesson from the failure, thus foiling your replication of the same mistake, I'll be far from ecstatic. One day, Sophia showed me a contract she had awarded a subcontractor about a year before. Recent commodity price changes revealed that during that year we had been paying too much. When I asked Sophia what happened, she said, "I don't know"—three little words I don't like hearing from anyone on my staff.

If she had said, "Drywall prices are rose from \$221/MSF to \$232/MSF, and we have been paying \$232/MSF because I forgot that Phoenix pricing should be much lower than Southern California pricing," I would have been pleased. A lesson learned is usually worth the cost of the failure. Creating a culture where it's okay to fail can liberate employees to realize their full potential and represent your company well, instead of them trying to play it safe or sweep mistakes under the rug.

A COMMON LANGUAGE WILL BIND YOU

For a purchasing department only utilizing lump-sum pricing, converting to unit pricing entails a great deal of hard work and discovery. But once implemented, unit pricing makes their jobs easier. So reward everyone for their tenacity by making requests or asking for reports that show the rich benefits of the new system, illustrating how their hard work has paid off while emanating your own amazement and delight.

For example, when the department gets unit pricing in place, yet someone on the senior staff asks them to convert cost reports back to lump-sum pricing, this lack of awareness and ineffectual management will knock the wind out of their sails.

Instead, ask for something that previously would have proved impossible. For instance, ask them for a lumber report showing how much you are paying per lumber SKU (i.e., 2"x4", 2"x6") for each community as well as a histogram of your composite lumber costs over the past three years, overlaid with data from your lumber commodity price tracker. For unit pricing to remain sustainable in your company, unit pricing language must resonate company-wide. Oh, yeah, that's the question you want to ask —not a question about how much concrete is costing us per square foot. (concrete unit pricing is: per cubic yard)

TRAINING: NO MORE WINGING IT

Until now, all your purchasing and construction personnel have been winging it. They've probably received no formal training for the work they're currently performing yet could greatly benefit from a consistent training program, whether outsourced or in-house.

And here's a key aspect: Ensure your staff all get the same training. Alignment on methodology creates a culture of unity, making employees feel confident they're doing the right thing. Your subcontractors, distributors, and manufacturers will recognize your employees' alignment and make an effort to conform to your culture. Without this alignment, a supplier's attempts to try to adapt to the nuances of each employee they encounter would prove futile if each cites or portrays a slightly different spin on "who we are." Train to align with strategic objectives and desired cultural characteristics. Don't bother trying to acquire higher-skilled people from another homebuilder; they don't have a training program either.

KNOCK DOWN THE OFFICE BARRIERS

My experience working with builders and suppliers in Japan has provided a welcomed addition to my toolbox of best practices. I was stationed in Japan on three occasions: twice as a builder and, finally, in a three-year position in Yokohama, Japan, as a building inspector/project manager. I managed the Japanese contractors that did work on our military bases. As I write this book, my company represents US building material manufacturers in several countries, including Japan, giving me opportunity to travel there about six times a year. I've learned much from them.

As a company grows, it becomes more and more challenging to master the art of internal communications. The larger the company, the more siloed their departments become, and things begin to slip through the cracks. Interestingly, the Japanese business culture mitigates this tendency: no offices, no cubicles, no barriers.

In a typical Japanese office, the desks or tables are placed next to each other without barriers. Any divider that might be in place is set low enough so your view of all your colleagues remains unobstructed, completely free and clear, without you having to stand up. In the US, this kind of close working environment could take some acclimation, but the benefits are worth it. Whenever you're are on a phone call in Japan, the whole office can potentially hear every word. So they're brought up to speed on what's going on, as it's happening. Employees might not purposely listen in on your phone call, but if even partially heard, your conversation effectually disseminates the information in real time. Each employee picks up on needed information from many of the calls and interoffice discussions, aligning them on everything happening and making formal meetings practically unnecessary.

Japan is not the only place to use this strategy; it's catching on in the US as well. I have toured the corporate offices of Google, Nike, WeWork, Starbucks, Amazon, and Airbnb in recent years and have concluded that the days of the cubicle are coming to a close. The openness offered in the less encumbered office spaces allows real-time collaboration to occur naturally, giving people a more satisfying feeling of connectedness.

If you conduct all your dealings with subcontractors and suppliers in a closed office, then you must report all pertinent information to all those that can benefit. Offices and cubicles with high walls can prove a hindrance to effective communication, making sustained, significant changes in supply chain management a little harder to achieve.

GET THEM OUT OF THE OFFICE

When I first took over as a purchasing manager, I visited many of our subcontractors' offices. I wanted to know what it was like to do business with us—*from their perspective.* I had some terrific conversations with their staff and was constantly amazed by an important takeaway: They talk to you quite differently when you're in *their* office instead of them being in yours. Much to my chagrin, these visits spawned many good ideas for making changes to the supply chain, yet my boss failed to grasp the value of what I was learning—how it translated into tremendous cost savings for our company. No matter what I showed him, he felt it was best if I just stayed in my office and did my job. Woe to the short-sighted thinking of this perspective.

Your supply chain management team will learn far more from visits to the job site and to your subcontractors' and suppliers' offices than they ever will from their desks. Compel them to get out of the office for at least a few hours each week. They will discover opportunities to drive efficiency, many of which will turn into cost savings. They will also build rapport and mutual respect with those they visit. Nearly all the people I visited in the first few years said I was the only homebuilder who ever visited them. "They always make us come to them," the subcontractors lamented.

Your subcontractors and suppliers don't care how much you know until they know how much you care. This phrase sounds like it belongs on a greeting card, I know, but read it once more and drink in its wisdom. Once I started communicating the value of my visits, our division president made it a policy that he visit every subcontractor once a year. And how did the subcontractors respond? Like the president of the United States himself had visited them—in the flesh. They often took pictures and put the photos on the wall for all to see. Bottom line: Don't underestimate the value of spending time with the folks entrusted with managing the most significant expense of your business—construction labor and building materials.

ALL OPS ON-BOARD

Reflect with me a moment on the story I told you about one of the homebuilding companies that had trouble sustaining a supply chain management transformation. This company had made the mistake of calling it a "purchasing initiative," a phrase used in staff meetings, monthly reports, and internal emails. Words matter, and these words told the whole company to ignore what was happening unless you were in the purchasing department.

Yet supply chain management touches nearly every department of a homebuilding company, especially the construction and customer service departments. To sustain a supply chain transformation, even if just a pilot program, you must include the entire operations team, which typically consists of purchasing, construction, and customer service, as well as the entire senior staff. Show your commitment to this new way of doing business by integrating the appropriate language in all your internal communications. The use of the right words is an indispensable element of a culture to support a rapidly changing supply chain team.

CULTURE = CHARACTER

The culture of a company is similar to the character of a person. You've probably heard character loosely defined as "the things a person does *when they know no one is looking*." Likewise, the way employees in a company behave *when they know no one will find out* is a reflection of that company's culture.

Development of a person's character happens slowly over time, and changing that character is like turning an oil tanker: slow and steady. Character is predominately made up of a person's habits. It's difficult to change your character, but less of a challenge to choose *one habit* to break.

Habits are formed from repeated behaviors. It's easier to change behaviors than habits.

Behaviors are developed from repeated actions. It's easier to change an action before it becomes in inherent behavior, and it's impossible to have an action without it first being a thought to incite that action.

If you want to be more in control of your actions, you must first control your thoughts. Our thoughts are stimulated by several things: books, TV, movies, social media, Internet videos, friends, family, neighbors, and more.

So, what's the easiest way to control the quality of your character? *Control the stimulus allowed into your mind*, which forms your thoughts, which incites an action.

The culture of your company was formed in a similar way. Habits and behaviors of employees are on display—through every internal interaction and every external touchpoint. The culture is exemplified by the thoughts and actions of every employee. These thoughts and actions are stimulated by input from its leadership, which can deliberately steer the culture in a particular direction or unintentionally prod the culture in another direction.

Companies successful in sustaining long-term cost reductions make it a practice to weave the supply chain strategy through nearly every department. Sales and marketing departments can co-brand with materials or services that add value to the homebuyer. Project management and land development leverage the lower costs (to get more land deals) as well as the unit pricing (to more accurately predict future costs). The accounting department aligns its processes with the new way of contracting, including the potential of buying more materials directly. Most of all, the construction, purchasing, and customer service departments need to embrace a new way of doing things. Make supply chain strategies part of your unique culture, and the cost savings are sure to prove sustainable long-term.

MANAGING THE GRIEF OF CHANGE

In her book *On Death and Dying*, [28] Elisabeth Kubler-Ross introduces us to the five stages of grief as part of the natural cycle a person goes through when experiencing the death of a loved one. I have adapted these five stages of grief as a tool to help people manage the process of change.

The five stages are denial, anger, bargaining, depression, and acceptance. When a subcontractor is asked to use builder-supplied materials, here's an example of what he may say to himself:

Denial – I can't believe the builder is making us do this! None of the other builders are doing it. Let's ignore their request and see if they forget about it, or maybe they'll ask someone else. Oh, no, they're asking us again. Keep ignoring them. Uh, oh, they're calling me now. I'll tell them I'm working on it. The stall may cause them to forget about it.

Anger – They're just trying to take away what little profit we're making and keep it for themselves. Now, they're asking for the amount we will deduct from our contract. Don't give them the real price; let's keep some of it. If it doesn't make sense financially, they'll go back to the old way of doing things. Maybe we don't want to work for this builder anymore; it's time to start looking for work with other builders.

---

[28] Elisabeth Kubler-Ross, *On Death and Dying* (New York: Simon & Schuster, Inc., 1969).

Bargaining – Ask the builder if we can try this in only one community. Let's ask them if we can just try it out for a little while and then go back to the old way. Ask the builder if we can keep the profit we would have made on selling the materials, and we'll give the builder the price of just the material, not including our markup. Let's ask the builder to provide us with contracts on more communities if we agree to do this.

Depression – Well, it looks like we have to do this. This is going to be terrible. I hate my job. This is going to make me look like a fool. My peers will laugh at me. I'm never going to make money with this builder again. This sucks!

Acceptance – We don't have to buy those materials anymore, so I have more money for cash flow to support my payroll. The builder is giving us more communities, so that means more business, more revenue, lower expenses, which equates to higher profit margins. I'll never have to worry about the theft of those materials again. The new process is so easy; I can't believe they could be so good at this so quickly. This is going to work out nicely. I love working for these guys.

I guarantee you are going to experience every one of these emotions with your subcontractors and suppliers. Some subcontractors go through the five stages slowly and painfully. Some fly through them and arrive at the acceptance stage before you realized they were even in denial. Sometimes, a subcontractor will stay in the denial stage for months and then suddenly fly through the remaining four stages. Also, the first four stages don't have to come in any particular order, and people may weave back and forth between them. Don't fight it; everyone processes change a little differently. If you recognize they will be experiencing these emotions, you can prepare to help them along. Do not deny their feelings, just help them through the stages.

When you see a subcontractor in the denial stage, you may want to tell him how much you value doing business with him and that *this new process will bring us closer together*. Perhaps say, "If I do this with another subcontractor, you may miss out on a great opportunity." Tell him, "I want you on the winning team, and this new process is going to set us all apart."

A subcontractor in the anger stage may benefit from hearing that you're not out to steal his profit. Reiterate why you are doing this: "We're going to reduce the cost to build a house so more people can afford to buy a home, keeping us all employed for another day."

A subcontractor in the bargaining stage, like a desperate plea for leniency, will come up with all kinds of ideas to mitigate his perceived fears. The first few times I asked a subcontractor to use builder-supplied materials, I let her keep the profit she would have made. We agreed to do this for some time; then we removed it from her contract after we were both comfortable with the process and confident in what to expect from a new sense of normal.

A subcontractor in the depression stage needs to hear how good things are going to be. Acknowledge her grief, then reiterate some of the potential advantages. Let her know, that you won't let her fail, that this needs to work for both of you, and that you're in it together.

I've kept the five stages of grief written on the whiteboard in my office for most of my career. My staff and I would often roleplay how to help move people through these stages, including ourselves and internal colleagues, like the construction department. Change is difficult for everyone. When you recognize this and anticipate that they will go through the five stages of grief, you are creating a culture that will support the long-term sustainability of a robust supply chain management program.

A NEW DEFINITION OF TEAM

Large homebuilding companies have a purchasing department responsible for executing all the subcontract agreements and change orders, as well as procuring materials. They are responsible for managing a homebuilder's most significant expense. The purchasing manager sits in on budget meetings where cost overruns are discussed. Solutions for reducing costs are brainstormed by the purchasing department and sometimes vetted with the construction department. It's not common to bring people from outside a homebuilding company to participate in budget meetings . . . until now.

A clever purchasing manager will involve his subcontractors in solving cost issues. Magical things happen when you make subcontractors feel like they're part of the team. Idea generation between the purchasing department and subcontractors working together as a team will produce unique opportunities. As they continue working together, the ideas will get better and better.

Eventually, though, you will run out of ideas that create enough savings, and that's when the subcontractors will begin to throw up roadblocks for further cost reduction, so beware. They'll bring up issues with their suppliers, using distributors as a constraint.

The next logical approach for the clever purchasing manager is to bring the subcontractor in with his distributor—completely new territory for the distributor. Make the distributor feel like he's part of the team as well, and he will combine his knowledge, skills, and resources to further the efforts to reduce costs. If you discover an uncooperative distributor and have tried everything to win him over but he just doesn't want to join the team, consider replacing him. Do all you can first, but it's easier to give birth than to resurrect the dead (an apt saying here, when you think about it). If you have a distributor that rejects the team player mindset, you may have to let him go.

Your subcontractors' distributors can present many concerns that affect pricing. Distributors control the logistics of bringing materials to their warehouse from manufacturers, as well as the logistics of delivering products to the job sites. Several aspects of their internal operations also contribute to higher pricing. Help the distributor solve his issues, and the price can come down. If you're successful in making him feel part of the team, like his needs are important to you, he will offer up pricing concessions—slowly at first—but then, as he sees your commitment to helping him become more efficient, he will lower his prices more.

At some point, however, when you have exhausted his more obvious cost concerns, he will likely bring up the manufacturer as part of the problem.

That's when the purchasing manager recruits the manufacturer to also join the team to reduce costs so more people can afford to buy a home. When you convince the manufacturer that his needs are important to you, that you're not just standing with your hand out for alms but want to make his job easier so his operating costs will decline (producing lower prices to the distributor), he will be happy to climb onboard. Until this point, the only contact you likely have with the manufacturer is concerning the collection of rebates in exchange for your promise to use his products. Yet I've found that manufacturers value being part of a homebuilder's team. They rarely get asked, and their offers to help usually get brushed off as empty talk.

Through this process, the purchasing manager will realize that when he imagines his subcontractors' personnel as his own employees, empathy will illuminate what he can do to help subcontractors become more efficient, lowering their cost of doing business so they can reduce pricing to the builder. The subcontractor wants help ensuring that the job is ready when his crews arrive, that all the resources are available to enable natural work completion, and that he gets paid quickly. Changes to construction schedules not communicated in a timely way and late options that interrupt the natural flow of his operations will both cost him money. Help him solve these issues, and his prices to you will begin to slide as well.

As the builder and subcontractor use the same process and invite the distributor under their umbrella—imagining they're all employees of the same company, just perhaps in different departments—then empathy will enlighten builders and subcontractors to the distributor's needs. The distributor makes money by increasing his number of inventory turns. It's his crucial metric. But because he doesn't know what a subcontractor plans to order until twenty-four to forty-eight hours before delivery, he over-inventories SKUs, just in case someone orders them. So when the builder and subcontractor work together to consistently notify the distributor thirty, sixty, or ninety days in advance, the distributor's cost of doing business decreases, and he can offer the subcontractor lower prices.

As a manufacturer is left in the dark—not knowing the what and when of SKUs needed—they must guess what to make and when to make it. This system produces unwanted inventory that costs the manufacturer money. In contrast, they are most efficient when they sell a product as soon as it comes off the assembly line. Any interruptions in that objective add to their cost of doing business. When the builder, subcontractor, and distributor rally to send demand signals, letting the manufacturer know which SKUs will be needed thirty, sixty, or ninety days in advance, manufacturers can operate at their highest capability and lower prices to the distributor.

When a purchasing manager gets to this point, it doesn't take him long to appreciate that he cannot fulfill the wishes of these supply chain partners without the construction superintendent. The superintendent sits at the helm, his fingers pushing the buttons that send signals for the product to be made, shipped, staged, and sent out on last-mile delivery. The team with the greatest ability to reduce the cost to build a house consists of a well-oiled lineup of like-minded players: the homebuilder, subcontractor, distributor, and manufacturer working together as one team with the shared goal of reducing the cost to build a house so more people can afford to buy homes. These people comprise your team. Knowing why you're linked together, focusing on an end goal and mission, proves more important than knowing exactly how each step will progress. Just keep telling them *why* you're all doing this together.

RIGHT PEOPLE ON THE BUS?

Managing costs requires a different skill than managing contracts. You may discover that your purchasing and construction personnel, though good at managing contracts, might not be so good at managing costs. Of course, it's always best when you can train your existing staff. Whether you teach them in-house or use an outsourcing agency, ensure they get trained. Training proves far less expensive than employee turnover.

Yet even if you shift personnel to other departments, a learning curve may bring an unfortunate cost. Be cautious not to hang onto the wrong employee for too long and thus lose out on some opportunities. For example, delaying the realization of increased profit margins may cost you more than it takes to find a good cost manager.

Besides managing costs, your purchasing and construction team may find it a new experience to work collaboratively with entities outside your company. Those teams that have collaborated with subcontractors only on a limited basis may need some additional training before they are ready to take on such a crucial task. But for builders who already collaborate with subcontractors exceptionally well, adding distributors and manufacturers to the mix should not require much, if any, additional training.

WE CALL IT THE PURCHASING DEPARTMENT, BUT IS IT?

My brother once had a cat named Mouse. Since the cat spoke no English, I don't think the cat was confused, but it sure entertained those who learned the cat's name. Had my brother named his son Cat, I think we would have had a much bigger issue on our hands. I'm hoping this brief story lets the cat out of the bag, so to speak, about the importance of words and how their use matters, specifically when it comes to the five disciplines comprising supply chain management. In small homebuilding companies, a person may wear multiple hats, but in large companies, numerous people may wear the same hat. So it's important to use proper terminology. Here's how I interpret the five disciplines of supply chain management for the homebuilding industry:

- Purchasing – Subcontracting labor and materials.
- Procurement – Directly procuring materials from a distributor or manufacturer.
- Logistics – Managing the ships, planes, and trucks required to move a product from the manufacturer to the distributor, to the subcontractor, to the job site.
- Strategic Sourcing – Strategically aligning your company with manufacturers for mutual benefit. Some large builders call it "National Contracts."
- Contract Management – Managing the transactional processes of assembling bid packages, getting contracts and change orders signed, and then tracking and filing them in compliance with established legal and ethical standards.

TECHNOLOGY TO SUPPORT SUPPLY CHAIN MANAGEMENT

Technology can be a supply chain manager's best friend or greatest foe. My secret weapon at Standard Pacific Homes was the talent in the IT department—three people who had IT experience from various manufacturing companies. When I told them we had to enable JD Edwards software to manage unit pricing and then send data to our supply chain partners, they said "no problem" and got it done fast. Within four months, we had computer-to-computer communication with one of our supply-chain partners.

One of the essential characteristics of supply chain collaboration? Consistency. SKU and Date Needed data remain key to significant cost reductions for our industry, but only if you can provide it consistently. Technology stands paramount to ensuring information flows to all the right people at the right time, *every time*. When you can provide that constant and reliable flow of information, you won't need to prod your supply chain partners to figure out what to do with it; they've been desperate for this information for a long time.

Your software and hardware options to support homebuilder operations are growing vastly in size and possible combinations every year. I'm a strong proponent of technology, which enabled nearly every one of my supply chain solutions. So don't be shy. Just as a hammer is to a carpenter, technology is to a supply chain manager. To make the cost reductions so badly needed in our industry, we need all supply chain managers to leverage the robust ability of today's technology solutions.

What tasks do supply chain managers need technology to solve? Here's a sample:

- Generate material take-offs from architectural drawings. Technology in this area gets better every year. My preference for most take-offs is to have the architects provide it with their construction drawings. Many architects are drawing in 3-D now, and with a little programming, you can teach the 3-D drawing objects how to count materials. Until that is perfected, however, some excellent estimating programs are available.
- Manage unit pricing in contracts and change orders. Contracts are managed in a company's back-office system, whether Quick Books or JD Edwards, and managing unit pricing is nothing more than making some programming changes. Whatever it takes, it's worth it.
- Distribute electronic construction schedules—a tool for the construction superintendent to manage his job and a communication tool for subcontractors and suppliers. Real-time updates are essential to communicating

effectively to all parties that need to know. When purchase orders are married with tasks on a construction schedule, it enables the SKU and Date Needed information to be viewed by those who need it.

- Produce electronic invoicing. When a superintendent checks off the task in the construction schedule as complete, ideally the system automatically pays the subcontractor or supplier. I'm happy to see paper invoices becoming a thing of the past.

- Boost customer service. Builders strive for high-quality homes, as measured by homeowner surveys and customer service calls. When supply chain managers consider the award of a contract, it's essential to include customer service calls in the report of how a subcontractor or supplier is doing.

- Provide a supplier scorecard. I'm an advocate of the supplier scorecard. Similar to a school report card, it lets the subcontractor know how they are doing from the perspective of the homebuilder's operations team.

FINAL THOUGHTS: MAKE SURE THEY KNOW WHY

When I was a platoon commander in the US Navy Seabees, I required each of my four squad leaders to always have with him a list of the people in his squad, complete with the following information: name, rank, serial number, blood type, hometown address, religion, weapon number, spouses'/children's names, hat size, boot size, shirt size, trouser size, local address, phone number, special training, and weapons qualifications. Keeping this list on hand was a serious matter, and if they were caught without it, they could be disciplined.

However, when I was a squad leader and had to carry around this information, I lamented its futility. What was the point? All could be found in a Seabee's records and some of it on his dog tags. So why carry around what seemed like duplicate efforts? I'm embarrassed to say I didn't figure it out until after my fourteen-year enlistment had ended.

A standard military order contains five parts: who, what, when, where, and how. *Why* is not part of a military order. And that makes sense. In a crisis, no one has the luxury of time to explain why. In a combat situation, the value of not explaining why seems obvious, and while I was questioning why we had to carry around a list of information, I knew my company commander wasn't obligated to tell me why. We just did what we were told.

The military leader who formulated the requirement for squad leaders to have this information for each member of his squad was a wise man. He knew that if Seabees were going to depend on each other in a combat zone, they could not wait until bullets were flying to get to know each other. The required list was intended to force squad leaders to get to know their people. You cannot take care of folks until you get to know them.

Sadly, we only did the minimum. We kept a list with the minimum information just so we could check the box to say it was complete. When a new guy joined your squad, you went down the list and got all his information so you wouldn't get in trouble. Had I known *why* we were doing it, I'm sure I would have embraced the spirit of the task and used it as a starting point—not an endpoint—to get to know my people. Ah, the opportunities lost.

Transforming a supply chain management strategy in a homebuilding company is much like being a pioneer. Not many of the paths are paved. Make sure that your team—*your new definition of team*—is continually reminded of why you're all doing this. When construction costs go down, home prices can go down, enabling more people to buy a home and keeping us all in business a little longer.

CHAPTER 11

Conclusion: From Cycle Time Reduction to Supply Chain Management

I can't help but reflect back on that Process Improvement Team meeting I described as your journey through this book began, the one where I found an invaluable tidbit of wisdom we had cast aside in our notes. Though I stumbled across a few words that I considered a priceless jewel, its wisdom wasn't applied for quite some time and certainly wasn't included in the results of that big three-day event.

Still, that momentous meeting provided the starting point for me. It launched me into the most amazing pursuit of my life—to find the real, practical solutions to uncover *your greatest cost savings in residential construction by listening to your suppliers.*

Yet I think it's worth understanding how that meeting eventually went down, the event that showcased the PIT team's most innovative solutions and the single most significant initiative our company had ever tackled. The cycle time reduction project included half the personnel in our company and most of our subcontractors—hundreds of people. And while my gut was telling me we would be successful in finding new, innovative solutions, it wasn't until much later that our eyes were opened to the real answers, the path that would lead to the beginnings of industry transformation.

But at that point, as we wrapped up that meeting, no one knew that the answer to construction cycle time reduction lay in better management of building materials. No one.

I was hired just one year before that event, not because of my production homebuilding experience—I didn't have any—but because of my Total Quality Management (TQM) training, an uncommon résumé to have for construction superintendents like me. But I was certainly in the right place at the right time when Shea Homes, San Diego, hired me. As it turned out, just as I had ended my fourteen-year career as a US Navy Seabee, Shea Homes was looking for TQM-qualified construction personnel. They only found one. Now, I had to prove they didn't make a mistake.

I seemed to fit in right away. The company was fully engaged with multiple consultants to train its employees in quality management. The training all looked familiar to me as the US Navy had deployed similar training during my enlistment. The Navy's motivation to do so was prompted by the infamous $600 hammer the US Navy was caught procuring. So, as you can imagine, eliminating waste became an all-hands direct order. US Navy Seabees perform construction on military bases around the world, and this directive gave me a chance to apply TQM training to construction operations.

But Shea Homes was not the Navy, and I was no longer a Seabee. It was time to find out if all that training was going to pay off in production homebuilding.

All of our superintendents were involved in this process at one point or another, but only three of us saw the project from beginning to end. This big event and PIT team initiative was an extracurricular activity; we still had our regular jobs to do. But getting caught up after missing three or four days would be worth the potential benefit, we believed. This project's objective was to reduce our ninety-eight day construction cycle time. We didn't know how far we could go, but our newly TQM-trained staff and senior management all had high expectations. Could we shave off ten days? How about twenty days? What was possible? We planned to push the limits of conventional construction practices and question everything. We figured extensive preparation would be paramount to our success.

This process may now be familiar to many homebuilders looking to improve business performance, but our TQM approach added nuances that made it unique. One of our TQM trainers was named Jack—a retired rocket scientist. One day in the office, Bruce, one of the TQM managers, introduced me to Jack by asking if we had met. I replied that we had not. Bruce said, "Oh, you don't know Jack?" and he walked away laughing his head off, continuing to do so all the way down the hall. Now, I know Jack, and I have Bruce to thank for it.

Jack's specialty was process mapping. First, he helped us identify every task, every step, every single thing we did at Shea Homes, and then he taught us how to create a precedence diagram, including who was responsible for accomplishing each step. This entire effort took about nine months with folks often at the office until ten o'clock at night. I was usually one of them. This process map of how to build a house would become part of our preparation for reducing construction cycle time.

We divided the construction schedule into six stages: foundation, framing, rough utilities, drywall, cabinets-trim-paint-flooring, and exterior. In each of these stages, all activities were identified by name, duration, and *predecessor* and *successor* activities—those that had to occur beforehand and those that could not occur until each one was complete. In evaluating our predecessor and successor activities, Jack would frequently ask, "What absolutely has to happen before this can occur?" If we didn't have a good answer, he would move the activity to a non-traditional place in the construction process.

For example, Jack noticed that "install windows" was on day forty-four after the roofing paper was installed. He asked something like, "Does the roof absolutely have to be papered before windows are installed?"

I said, "No, but that's the way we always do it." So Jack moved "install windows" to right after "exterior wall sheathing." Jack was not interested in "how we always do it." The result was a genuinely logic-based precedence diagram.

We sent the diagrams, construction schedules, and project objectives to our hand-selected subcontractors. Each was tasked to come to the meeting prepared to share their ideas on how to reduce the construction cycle time, relevant to the activities in the schedule under their responsibility.

All day long in the training room, each group would argue to take five days out, and then concede to put three back in. Or take three days out, put one back in. After hours of lively discussion, the group eventually concluded that taking any more days out of the schedule would negatively affect construction quality. We settled on this new standard and repeated the process for all stages of the construction schedule. The meetings for the first few stages lasted longer than subsequent stages—partly because the facilitating team got used to the process and functioned more effectively toward the end and partly because they just wanted to get it over with.

Thirteen hours per day for three and a half days had ended. It felt like three weeks. Three meals per day of catered food seems to have left an odor imprinted upon the room. More than one person used a permanent marker on a whiteboard, and their attempts to clean left big smears. Aside from how exhausted we all felt and the lasting wear on the training room, we were all satisfied with the outcome. I could not have anticipated how robust the efforts of our subcontractors would be—and all to help us improve our business. Each of them performed in exemplary ways.

The comradery that developed between the subcontractors and the homebuilder remained unprecedented. And because of this extraordinary team effort, we reached a newfound confidence in our ability to improve any process. Regardless of anyone's criticism of our performance, we felt we had done a great thing.

We circulated the innovative construction schedule to our operations team to serve as a second set of eyes and catch anything we may have overlooked. Inevitably, we ended up putting two days back in the schedule because someone found something that just wouldn't work. Now we had a construction schedule ready to publish to all our subcontractors, including those not part of the PIT team, for their review. To limit the amount of pushback we might get, we labeled it as "non-negotiable." After some robust debate from a few of them, we put two more days back in the schedule. "We need more time to do our jobs," they said.

We started with a ninety-eight-day schedule . . . and ended up with a ninety-four-day schedule. All those hours and months of toil had resulted in a four-day reduction. Was it worth it? I have to say "yes" . . . because it was just the beginning.

At the time we ended the project, we compared our innovative schedule with that of other builders and concluded we were among the best; it couldn't get any shorter. We ended the project. Whew!

But here's where even bigger benefits started pouring in. A by-product of the Cycle Time Reduction PIT team was the unreserved voice of the subcontractor. We were so focused on what would make our homebuilding operations more effective, we didn't stop to think about what we could do to make the subcontractor more effective, too. I guess we assumed that whatever we came up with, they would find an efficient way to deliver results regardless of what new requirements we threw at them.

Some of our subcontractors got wrapped up in the spirit of continual improvement. They voiced concerns that we should have been listening to long before. So this time, we heard. We encouraged them to be as forthcoming as this venue and assemblage would allow. I couldn't stop thinking about the subcontractors' cry for help. Helping them would help us too, wouldn't it? If we could facilitate a more efficient use of their workers' time, we might share in the benefits, including lower contract prices and shorter cycle times.

This PIT team triggered our eventual discovery that the secret to significant cycle time reduction was not having the right *person* in the right place, but having the right *materials* in the right place at the right time, *every time*. This ended up being worth a great deal more than the few days we took out of the schedule during that grueling three-day event. Learning to work together as a team would prove even more fruitful.

I'm a carpenter at heart, not a supply chain manager. Since the age of eleven, I've been driven by the gratification of seeing what I just made. I could never have imagined that the PIT team project and its subsequent discoveries would compel me to jump into the supply chain management role to improve construction operations.

But as we got started one material at a time—simply wanting to know *how much is the milk?*—we uncovered more and more opportunities for improvement. It seemed like every stone lifted unveiled four more stones. Collaborating with everyone in the supply chain to change the way our industry manages building materials ended up being one of the most satisfying things I've ever done.

I love the outdoors, hiking in the mountains, swimming in the ocean, and camping in the woods. I adhere strictly to the motto: Leave it better than you found it. In this light, those in this wonderful, purpose-filled industry can take the same mission to heart. Implementing all the tools in this book won't be easy; resistance from all angles may arise. Along the way, you will find folks who catch the spirit of continual improvement, who lock arms with you to leap the obstacles and learn from the mishaps to finish the race to the end. Nourish those relationships while striving to make the industry better for someone else, and you'll be leaving it better than you found it.

My deepest thanks to you for taking the time to read these pages and consider making their mission your own. Best to you in all your efforts.

—*Ken Pinto*

Printed in the USA
CPSIA information can be obtained
at www.ICGtesting.com
LVHW041932121123
763661LV00037B/1465/J